The Joy of Bocce

Mario Pagnoni

Masters Press
A Division of Howard W. Sams & Co.
A Bell Atlantic Company

Published by Masters Press (A Division of Howard W. Sams & Company, A Bell Atlantic Company)
2647 Waterfront Parkway East Drive, Suite 300
Indianapolis, IN 46214

10   9   8   7   6   5   4   3   2   1

Library of Congress Cataloging-in-Publication Data

Pagnoni, Mario.
        The joy of bocce / Mario Pagnoni.
            p.   cm.
        ISBN 1-57028-044-4 (pbk.)
        1. Bocce (Game)   I. Title.
    GV910.5.B63P35 1995   95-45633
    796.31--dc20   CIP

Acknowledgments

First and foremost, I must thank my father-in-law, Gennaro Daniele, who gave me my first set of bocce balls. This gift led to a love affair with the sport. After decades of baseball, basketball, jogging and three knee operations, bocce has become more appealing to me than ever.

Heartfelt thanks go to my son James, whose excellent photographs complement the bocce text so well. Thanks also to my son Joseph, who helped with the photo demonstrations and to my wife, Carmela who put up with the disaster area that our backyard became during the bocce court construction. My good friend Joe Austin deserves high praise and my undying gratitude for the many hours that he put into our backyard court construction.

Thanks also to Leonard Hickey who graciously submitted photos of bocce play at his marvelous, outdoor court in Wilbraham, Massachusetts.

For their input and objective criticism of early drafts of the manuscript my gratitude goes out to Donna Allen and Ken Dothée of the United States Bocce Federation, Rico Daniele of the Wonderful World of Bocce Association, and Phil Ferrari of the World Bocce Association. Special thanks to Jennifer Smith of Methuen who analyzed the manuscript from the perspective of a non-player.

Finally, many thanks to the good people at Masters Press including Tom Bast, Holly Kondras and Heather Seal. They embraced my idea for a book on bocce and, with great skill, took the project to completion.

Acknowledgements

Preface

Bocce, though already catching on rapidly in this country, would really take off if it got the proper exposure. Hopefully this book will help. I'm not talking about it flourishing as a tournament event with complicated rules, state-of-the-art equipment and high-powered authorities running (or ruining) the sport. I'm referring to a simplified recreational version that can be played by anyone almost anywhere. This game doesn't require great strength, stamina, quickness or agility. You don't need catlike reflexes or the hand-eye coordination of an NBA backcourt star. Men and women as well as boys and girls of all ages can participate and enjoy the sport, making it as competitive or as noncompetitive as they desire. And it is well-suited as a game for the countless physically-challenged individuals worldwide because anyone who can roll a ball can play. Best of all, you don't need expensive equipment. And, played as described here, you don't even need a court — your backyard or neighborhood park will do nicely. You can play recreational bocce on grass or dirt, on level or uneven terrain — even at the beach (on the shore or on sandbars during low tide).

Bocce suffers from an image problem in America. People see it as an "old fogies' game" played at social clubs. The word bocce conjures up images of cranky old coots competing on customized outdoor courts. Arguing and kibitzing (sometimes even cursing — usually in Italian) and generally having a great time, these old-timers seem engaged in some sort of geriatric lawn bowling. It looks about as exciting as watching cactus grow in the desert. But it is a wonderful game, full of skill and strategy — one that requires finesse as well as some occasional brute force. This book attempts to dispel the misconceptions about bocce, and aims to promote it as a lawn game that is the ideal recreation for family cookouts, picnics, and other get-togethers. In addition, this book helps guide those who may want to take the game to the next level, whether it be the social club level, tournament or international play. Most of all, our goal is to get the word out on what has been called "the best kept secret in sports," bocce.

Table of Contents

Chapter 1
The Game

The Reader's Digest Version (read this chapter and you're ready to play — come back later and read the rest of the book)

Bocce is a simple yet elegant game. Although I love the game as it is played in courts across the country and throughout the world, I'm partial to the simplified, backyard version — the one that can be played by men and women, boys and girls of almost any age. The one that can be learned in minutes and played almost anywhere. The one described in this chapter.

Bocce's Appeal

I am an unabashed promoter of bocce. I bring along a set of bocce balls when I travel or attend outdoor parties. Starting a game with family or friends on a patch of grass or dirt, we invariably draw a crowd. Inquiring people want to know — how do you play? What's the object? Are the balls just like bowling balls? Can I hold one to see how heavy it is? Most often they've heard of bocce before, but have seldom if ever played. After a five-minute explanation and a quick try, they're hooked. They want to know where to get their hands on a set of bocce balls and chances are good that they'll become instant BB's (Bocce Buffs).

Played the way we'll describe here, bocce is a gentle pastime, an entertaining recreational endeavor. Females should be pleased that in this age of male-dominated sports, bocce is suited equally to both sexes. Coed games are not only possible, but desirable. The tendency with backyard bocce is to include everyone — husbands and wives, neighbors, children — all want the ball in their court.

In subsequent chapters we'll take you through the terminology, examine the strategy, and tell you where to get equipment. We'll even describe how to construct a court of your own (if you have the inclination and the place to build one). There is also a brief bocce history lesson in store for you. But for now, here are the basics — enough for you to begin playing today.

Getting Down to Basics

A set of bocce balls consists of eight large balls and one small ball called the *pallino* (Italian for little ball). The larger balls are roughly the size of a grapefruit (the size, weight and composition vary with manufacturers and some offer a variety of sizes and weights to suit the individual player — see Chapter 5, The Equipment). Two teams compete against each other. Each team gets to roll or otherwise toss four of the larger balls toward the pallino (also called the jack, pill, or object ball). Each team's four bocce balls are of a different color or are otherwise marked for differentiation. For example, a set might consist of four red balls, four green balls and a yellow pallino. The object of the game is to score points by getting your team's balls close to the pallino. Novices think it advantageous to hit the pallino, but this may or may not be true. In any case, you don't score by hitting the pallino, but by directing your bocce balls closer to it than your opponents can. After both teams throw all of their balls, the frame or round is completed, and only one team will score. You score one point for each ball that is closer to the pallino than the closest ball of your opponent (to the pallino). Score one point if your ball is closest to the pallino, two points if you have the two closest to the pallino, etc. In this way, you can score up to four points in each round or frame. Presently there exists no standardization to the game; it is played differently all over the world (this may change rapidly as bocce becomes a Special Olympic sport and perhaps an Olympic event). The equipment can differ, as can the courts, rules, and even the winning score. The game can continue to 11, 12, 15, 16 or even 21 points (or another score that is mutually acceptable to the participants). We suggest games of 12. This is sufficiently long to make for fair competition, yet doesn't keep the on-deck players waiting too long (there are always on-deck players). Note: Although there are variations

One point

Two points

Three points

Four points

to the rules played around the country, a serious attempt to establish a standard set of "open" or "recreational" rules has been made by groups such as the United States Bocce Federation. Rules for international play are well established, having been used worldwide for years. These will govern future Olympic games, but are far more disciplined and complicated than the recreational rules discussed here (see chapter 9 for international rules).

The game is best played with one, two, or four players per team. In the one-on-one version (singles), each player rolls four balls. With two players per team (doubles), each participant tosses two balls. And the four vs. four game allows one roll for each team member. This last method of play has its ups and downs. On the plus side, it involves eight people at once. On the negative side, you only get one shot per frame (you do more watching than playing), and this prevents you from getting a feel for the terrain on any given lie.

With four-player teams there are two different formats. You can roll one ball each, as described above, with all eight playing from the same starting location. After the frame or round, the eight players walk to the other end of the court or play area and begin play back in the opposite direction. Of course, in your backyard or playground area (sans court) you can play in any direction you choose. We prefer to roll the pallino right from where we just completed the round, rather than picking up the balls and moving to a new starting point.

The alternate format is to station four participants (two from each team) at either end of your play area. With this method, each participant tosses two balls and stays at his end. We are basically dividing the teams of four into two subgroups of two. When the group from one end plays, the other group members act as coaches, fans, and probably most importantly — measurers. We keep a cumulative score — if you score two points and then your partners score two points, you are ahead four to nothing. We like games of 12, but as stated earlier, contests to 11, 15, 16, and even 21 are commonly played.

Two-on-two (doubles) is my favorite way to play bocce. You get two shots, allowing you to "go to school" on your first ball, and you get a partner allowing for greater camaraderie. After each frame you walk to the other end, pick up the balls and begin play in another direction. There is no reason you can't play with three players per team. You have to decide who on each team will get the extra ball each frame. Perhaps you could rotate it. You could even keep the six active by stationing four players at one end (two bocce balls each) and two at the other (four balls each). But with six or more players I prefer three teams of two in a kind of round robin format. Play games of 12 and have the on-deck team have a burger or act as measurers or referees. Depending on the skill of the participants, games last anywhere from 15 minutes to an hour. Another option with three- or four-player teams is to utilize two sets of balls so that each player can deliver two balls. Three player teams would require six balls per team (12 balls in play), so, theoretically, a team could score six points in one round. It might be advisable to set the winning score to a correspondingly higher total. Similarly, two four-player teams with two balls each make a total of 16 balls in play (with the possibility of eight points per frame). We suspect things will get pretty crowded — you might want to rethink this option.

To begin the game, teams must agree on who will toss the pallino first. You might flip a coin, throw fingers in the old odds-evens game of our youth, or come up with another alternative. The game starts when one player tosses the pallino to any position he desires. In our backyard bocce version there is no minimum or maximum distance that the pallino must be tossed (unless the players agree to such restrictions beforehand). Now the person who tossed the pallino must toss the first bocce ball, attempting to get as close to the pallino as possible. While you don't get points for hitting the object ball, a shot that nestles right up to pallino, obscuring it from the next player's sight, is very tough to beat. In any case, once the first ball is played, that team has the advantage — they're closest. Now it is up to the opponents to throw their bocce balls until they win the point — by getting closest to the pallino — so far. This may take one, two, three, or all four balls. Play continues in this manner (sometimes referred to as the nearest ball rule) until all balls are played and one team scores one, two, three, or four points. To recap — when Team A has the point (has the closest ball, or is "in"), they step aside and wait until Team B beats that point (has the in ball). Team B throws as many balls as needed to "outlag" Team A's ball. If they can do it with one ball, fine. Now it will be their point, and team A has to try to beat Team B's point. Obviously, a good first shot could force the opponents to use two, three, or even all four of their balls. This puts the team with a good first-point man (or woman) in an advantageous position.

Note: After the initial toss of the coin and subsequent first round of play, the team that scores always throws the pallino. Also, the player who tosses pallino must play the first ball as well. Teammates may decide among themselves who will toss pallino, or they may alternate this privilege, but the honor must go to someone on the team that scored.

Sometimes a shot is so close that it is too difficult to outlag. In this case a team is likely to try to knock it away with either a fast rolling shot called a *raffa* or a direct hit on the fly called a *volo*. In either case, successfully knocking away a close ball opens up the play for you or your teammate to come in for the point. As you will see in subsequent chapters, this movement of opponents' balls, your own team's balls, or even the pallino makes for an infinite variety of possible tactics.

Order of Play Within a Team

In singles play each player tosses four balls, so play proceeds quite simply. If your opponent is "in," it's your shot next. But with two or more players per team you need to decide which player will shoot when your opponents have the point. You might agree ahead of time that "I'll throw the first two balls and you throw the last two." In four-person teams (one ball to be played by each) you can also preset the order of throwing by designating a first, second, third, and fourth shooter. But most often teams will discuss strategy while the game is in progress and agree, "You are better at this type of shot — why don't you try it?" The only restriction is that whichever team has the point (has the nearest ball) — a player from the other team must play next.

On bocce courts, lines are marked to indicate how far forward players may stand when rolling a ball. And since courts are lined by sideboards, this limits players' lateral movement. But there are no such restrictions in an open backyard play area. Usually this doesn't present a problem — players agree to take their shots from the same general area. Sometimes disagreements arise when a number of balls are in front of the object ball and the shooter doesn't have a clear view of it. He takes a step to his right. Then another. And another. Clearly there has to be some limit or he could circle completely around to the other side of the balls. Try to get everybody to play from a couple steps left or right of where the object ball was thrown. If this doesn't work out, put down a welcome mat and instruct all to place one foot on the rug when taking their shots.

The Playing Surface

Although bocce is played worldwide on enclosed clay or dirt courts, you can play on almost any surface. You need only a dirt or grassy area of 30 to 70 feet long by at least eight feet in width. It may be perfectly level, extremely hilly or anywhere in between. In fact, sloping areas on the playing field make for interesting shots involving "reading the green" as in golf. Generally, good golfers make good bocce players. They're skilled at gauging just how far a ball might break to the right or left and they tend to have a soft touch (smooth release of the ball). Basketball players with a good shooting touch also tend to make good bocce players. They know how to let the ball roll off the fingertips imparting a forward spin to the ball (12 o'clock to 6 o'clock rotation).

Just as the enclosed court introduces a dimension of playing off the side and endboards, playing on the green (or dirt) adds a nifty element. You can toss the object ball in one direction, play a round, and then proceed in any other direction. You might roll the pallino near the base of that willow tree and see if you can navigate over, around or through the exposed roots. Or you could place it near that chain link fence (acting as a kind of sideboard) and try to carom shots, first kissing the ball off the fence, then steering it neatly next to the object ball. The possibilities are endless.

In backyard lawn bocce, most people play a kind of anything-goes style. Players tell of games during family cookouts where the pallino got knocked onto the picnic table and into a trash can. Rather then retrieve the object ball and start over, they proceeded to toss their balls as close to the barrel as possible (or even into it on the fly). You can be like Michael Jordan and Larry Bird...off the garage, through the clothes line, around the bird feeder, next to the pallino!

Measuring for Point

Measuring to find out which ball is closest to the pallino can present problems. At the most noncompetitive level of recreational bocce, players often concede a point on a close call or just agree to call it a tie (no point scored). At the opposite end of the spectrum, participants use state of the art measuring devices complete with calipers capable of discerning fractions of an inch.

The first rule in determining the nearest ball is to always move up to the area of the pallino. Sometimes a ball that appears to be inches away when viewed from the foul line is actually feet away when seen up close. And different angles can fool you. For example, Team A's first roll may end up about even with, but a foot or two to the right of the pallino. Team B's shot is straight on, but apparently six inches or so short of the pallino. Before Team A plays the next ball, they should get a better look by walking up to the balls and surveying the situation. Quite often the ball that appears to be six inches short is actually several feet short. Of course, this trip to the pallino area is unnecessary if you have someone acting as referee. A second important rule for determining which ball is in is to

 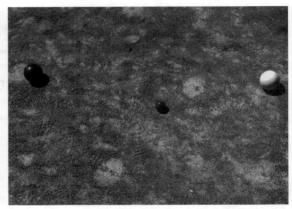

When determining point, always move up to the pallino and stand in the proper position. Sometimes a ball that appears from the foul line to be inches away is actually farther when seen up close. (See also drawing page 7)

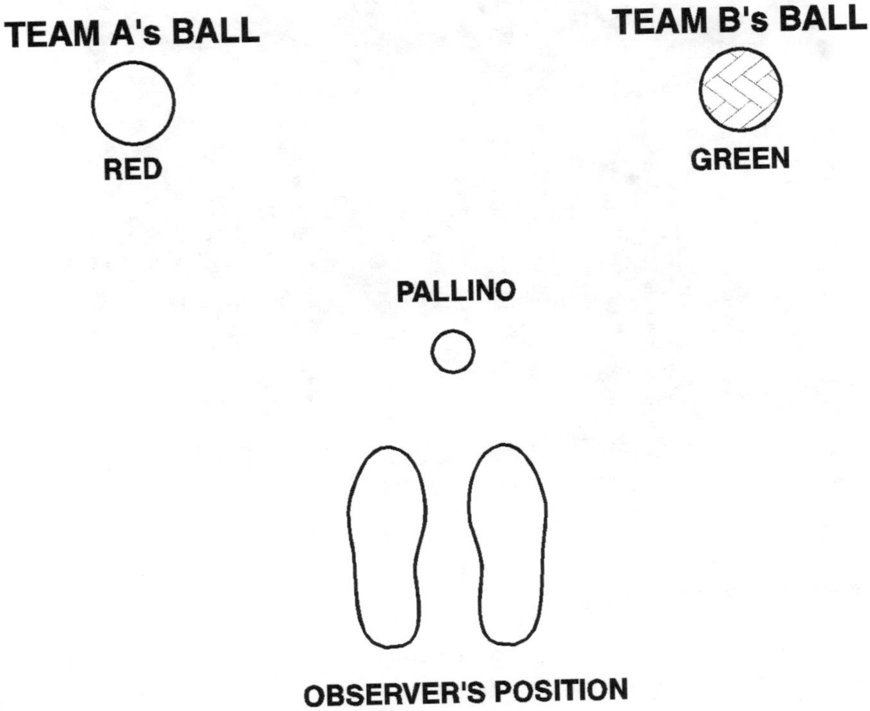

TEAM A's BALL

TEAM B's BALL

RED

GREEN

PALLINO

OBSERVER'S POSITION

stand behind the object ball in a kind of straddling position with the balls that are in contention in clear view (see photos previous page and drawing above). Experienced players using this method can determine which ball is in even when only fractions of an inch separate the balls.

My family and I have enjoyed backyard bocce for many years measuring only by eye or with feet, hands, and fingers. This nifty system really works! Start at the pallino and place the heel of your foot against it. Take care not to displace the pallino. Take "baby steps" straight toward the ball you are measuring, carefully placing the heel of one foot directly in front of the toe of the previous. When you get too close to the bocce ball to squeeze in another foot, keep your front foot in place, and kneeling down, use your fingers as more precise units of measure. In this way we can tell that the ball that is three feet and four fingers away is out, and the one that is three feet and three fingers away is in.

When the distances to be measured are smaller than feet and awkward for fingers, or require a bit more precision, we have used twigs, pieces of string, and other easily accessible objects. A telescopic radio, television, or car antenna works very well if it is sturdy and straight. A standard tape measure is helpful, especially for very long measurements. We have seen some neat homemade measurers, too. One creative guy on the bocce tournament circuit taped a car antenna and a presentation pointer together so that they could be opened telescopically in opposite directions. "A single antenna is good" he claims, "but it's just not long enough for many measurements." Finally, there are some precise measuring devices on the market which we outline in Chapter 5, The Equipment.

Utilizing a tape measure to determine point

Some Points on Measuring for Point

1. Stand by the pallino and see if you can make the call by eye. Give opponents a peek and see if you can come to an agreement.

2. Be extremely careful not to displace the pallino or bocce balls during measuring. If you do move a ball and cannot agree on its placement, it is good form to award the point to the team not responsible for the illegal movement. Some players like to secure the object ball's position by pressing down on it during measurement.

3. To score a point, a ball has to be closer to the pallino than the other team's ball. A tie just doesn't cut it. If, when the frame is completed, you determine that the closest balls rolled by Team A and Team B are tied (equal distance from the pallino), no points are scored. These balls do not cancel each other out and make the next closest ball a point. Again, no points may be scored when the two closest balls are from opposite teams and are equidistant from the object ball.

4. If one, two, or three points are sure, and two opposing team's balls are the next closest to pallino and tied, the previously determined points are scored, but the tied balls cancel each other out.

5. Tape measurements (metric units are always preferable to English) are sometimes made from the bocce ball to the center of the pallino. Instruct one person to place the end of the tape measure at the middle (equator) of the bocce ball, and direct another to extend the tape over the top center of the pallino and to read the result. This method requires a little estimation on the part of the measurer in terms of interpreting just where the center of the pallino is. The method is adequate, but can cause problems when two measurements are very close. Some players prefer to measure from the outer dimensions of the balls, but the best and most accurate way to determine which ball is in is with inside measure. You want to know which ball has the smaller amount of space between it and the pallino. Hold the tape measure or other device in between the two balls, measuring from the middle (equator) of one to the middle of the other. (See photo next page) Then move to the other ball in contention and compare your two findings.

One player handling a measurement alone   *Example of an inside measurement*

Play Ball!

Now you know enough to play. Give it a shot and come back and read some more later. In some rounds you may have difficulty telling which ball is closest to the object ball. Remember to get the best angle for determining which ball is in by standing by the object ball. If you cannot make the call by eye, you will have to resort to measurement. In subsequent chapters, we'll take you deeper into the strategy and finer points of play. For now, you know enough to go out and enjoy this great and ancient game.

The Romans played with somewhat rounded stones 2000 years ago. You can play with an inexpensive set of bocce balls or even your candlepin bowling balls (just to try out the game). Trent Formaggioni of Springfield, Massachusetts told me that as a child he played with eight softballs and a golf ball or baseball. "We used markers to differentiate each team's softballs, and we played on the grass at our neighborhood park." Recently, he competed in the World Cup of Bocce held in the Imperial Ballroom of Atlantic City's Trump Plaza. "I love the game — on both levels!" he proclaims with joy.

Dozen Steps To the Joy of Bocce

1. Secure a set of bocce balls, a place to play and some players.
2. Make two equal teams. One-, two- or four-person games are most common.
3. Toss a coin or otherwise select who will play first.
4. The team that wins the coin toss pitches the pallino and then rolls the first bocce ball, trying to draw as near as possible to the pallino.
5. The starting team stands aside and does not bowl again until the opposing team gets one of their bocce balls closer to the pallino or runs out of bocce balls.
6. Play proceeds in this manner, observing the nearest ball rule. The team with the nearest ball stands aside and waits until such time that the other team has the nearest ball or has used up all its balls in the attempt. Remember — the team that is in delays — the team that is out plays.
7. After both teams deliver all balls, the frame or round is over. Score one point for each ball that is closer to the pallino than the closest ball of your opponent.
8. The team that scores the point(s) starts the next frame by rolling the pallino and the first bocce ball.
9. Games can be played to 11, 12, 15, 16, 21 points, or to any mutually agreeable count.
10. Balls can be tossed underhand or overhand, through the air or bowled along the ground.
11. Think ahead — like chess. Possible strategies include knocking an opponent's ball out of scoring position, redirecting the pallino toward your previously played balls, and leaving a ball short of the pallino to block your opponent's attempt.
12. Have fun with this wonderful and ancient pastime — the best kept secret in sports.

Chapter 2
The Terminology

It helps to know what you are talking about

The terms that follow are listed alphabetically. Rather than a technical glossary, this section is designed in an easy-to-read format. It will familiarize the reader with words and situations that are used throughout the rest of the text. A brief perusal of these will set the stage for a clearer understanding of the chapters that follow. From *bank shot* to *winning score*, this sampling of bocce jargon will get you rolling in the right direction. Keep in mind that there is a difference between the way the game is played in recreational and tournament settings and the way it is played in true international competition.

bank shot - when playing on courts compete with side and backboards, a shot caromed off the side and/or backboard (illegal in some international play).

Sequence of a bank shot

bocce - sometimes spelled bocci or boccie - can refer to the balls used in the game or the game itself (e.g. players roll their bocce balls while enjoying a game of bocce). The balls can be made of wood, plastic, or composite material. Each of the eight balls in a set is four to five inches in diameter and weighs about two pounds. One team's bocce balls are distinguished from another's by color (e.g. four green balls, four red balls, and a smaller object ball or pallino of another color). In some sets, balls of the same color are inscribed with distinctive engraving so that teammates' balls can be differentiated from each another. In international play the balls are often metallic (brass is common). Note: As stated earlier, the word bocce means the game and the implement used to play the game

A set of bocce balls

(much like baseball refers to the ball and the game). Purists don't refer to the game as bocce ball. It is improper to ask "Do you want to play bocce ball?" or "Are you entered in the bocce ball tournament?" This would be like going to the ice rink and asking if anyone wanted to play hockey puck. "Do you want to play bocce?" and "Are you entered in the bocce tournament" represent accepted usage. The word is also properly used in this manner: "Roll your bocce off the sideboard."

bocce court or bocce alley (sometimes called the campo) - the enclosed playing surface complete with side and endboards. The surface is usually a fine gravel, clay or stone dust. Occasionally, court surfaces are grass, indoor/outdoor carpet or other artificial material. Courts are generally 60 to 90 feet in length (90 feet for international competition). Though no standardization yet exists in America, we have seen some movement in that direction recently. WWOBA (Wonderful World of Bocce Association) based in Springfield, Massachusetts and WBA (World Bocce Association) out of Bensenville, Illinois have agreed on 76 feet in length and 10 to 12 feet in width. Sideboards are at

Bocce courts

least as high as the balls (8 to 12 inches recommended) and higher at both ends where high velocity shots are more likely to knock the pallino out of the playing area. The United States Bocce Federation strongly recommends 90 feet in length by 13 feet in width. These dimensions provide a court suitable for true international rules as well as for open recreational rules. See Chapter 7, Building a Backyard Court for more details on court dimensions and construction.

boules - the French word for the balls and their version of the game — also called or pétanque. The balls are metallic and much smaller and lighter than bocce balls. The object ball (*but* or *cochonnet*) is significantly smaller, too (on the order of a table tennis ball). The game of boules is played on dirt or gravel without side or endboards. It is difficult to play on grass because even closely cropped lawns are likely to obscure the tiny object ball. The game is very similar to bocce and it is not much of a stretch to accept that bocce, boules, and lawn bowling all had a common ancestor.

bowls - the English game of lawn bowling and the balls themselves. The balls are biased (weighted on one side) so hook shots are prevalent. The name bocce is sometimes used interchangeably with lawn bowling but, despite their similarities, they are two entirely different games.

court markings - when playing on an enclosed court, as opposed to a patch of grass or dirt, the court has lines as prescribed by rule (regulations vary from area to area). To begin a frame, the pallino must cross the half court mark which is 38 feet on a 76-feet court. A pallino toss short of this line must be picked up and rolled again. Some rules mandate a line at each end of the court 4 feet from the back or endboard across which the pallino may not pass on the initial toss. In other words, the playable area for the first toss of pallino is beyond the 38-foot mark and before the 72-foot line. While play progresses, the position of the pallino may change by being hit by another ball (intentionally or accidentally). It may come to rest beyond the 72-foot line, but it may never end up closer to the players than midcourt, or the frame is dead and must be played over. (In addition, some rules call for the pallino to come to rest a minimum of twelve inches from the side boards.)

dead ball - a disqualified ball. In outdoor, recreational bocce using the so-called "open rules," there is almost never a dead ball. In club and tournament play on enclosed courts, a ball may be disqualified if:

- there is a penalty such as a foot foul
- it leaves the court's playing surface
- it comes into contact with a person or object which is outside the court
- it hits the top of the court boards
- it hits the covering of the courts or any supports

doubles - the game of bocce played with partners (two against two). Each player rolls two balls.

end - see frame below.

endboards - on an official court, the backboards are at each end. Players often carom shots off the side and endboards in attempt to score points although some international rules prohibit play off the side and endboards. Rather than just a static backboard, most courts have an additional swinging or hanging board that serves to absorb the force of a hard shot and prevent a long rebound. The facing of these swinging boards is often covered with an absorbent material (old fire hose, rubber tubing, etc.). On long shots, this prevents a player from getting close to the pallino simply by smacking the endboard and relying on the rebound effect to bring the ball into scoring position. Rather, a more skillful shot involving smooth touch and release is required.

foul line - on official courts the line the player must stand behind when rolling his bocce ball. Many players move forward as they release the ball, using a three- or four-step delivery as in tenpin or candlepin bowling. The ball must be released before the player passes the foul line. Some rules specify two foul lines — especially for play on shorter courts. For example, many 60-foot courts have a pointing line four feet from each end and a shooting or hitting line nine feet from each end. Many players take several steps in their approach when trying to hit a ball away. This would not be

Foul lines for pointing and hitting are indicated on the sideboard

possible without a longer runway to work with. On the other hand, this longer runway would bring the player too close to his target while attempting to close in for a point, so he would have to deliver his ball from behind the four-foot line when pointing. Some groups who play on longer courts approve one foul line for both pointing and hitting, reasoning that the greater distance makes the pointing line unnecessary.

fouls (also foot fouls, foot line fouls) - violations of the rules caused by a player stepping over the pointing line or hitting line before the ball leaves the player's hand. Players may not step over the foremost part of the line with any part of the foot before the ball leaves the hand. Some sets of rules call for one warning on a foot foul. Subsequent fouls carry penalties.

frame - also end or round; The period of time during which players from both teams roll their bocce balls from one court end to the other and points are awarded — similar to an inning in baseball or softball. When points are tallied, the frame is completed. If one point is scored each frame and the winning score is twelve, the contest will last twelve frames. Unlike baseball or softball, with games of nine or seven innings, the number of frames played in bocce is not predetermined.

hitting (see also raffa) - Rolling the ball with great force to displace a ball or balls, also shooting, spocking, popping, bombing. Since players often use a two-, three-, or four-step delivery for this shot, they may advance to the second foul line (hitting or spocking line) for this shot. The ball must be released before the foot crosses the foul line. Some rules define a spock or hit attempt as a throw with speed sufficient enough that it would hit the backboard if it missed its target. This is not always a satisfactory definition since, with fast, hard-packed court surfaces, it doesn't take a forceful roll for a ball to reach the backboard. In other words, a missed point attempt may hit the endboard and, by the letter of the law, it would be a spock or hit attempt.

initial point - the first ball thrown toward the object ball becomes the in ball and establishes the initial point. It is always incumbent on the team with pallino advantage to establish the initial point.

in - closest to the pallino. "Our team's ball is in so your team must play the next ball."

lag - also pointing; to roll for point. To deliver the bocce ball as close to the pallino as possible.

live ball - any ball that has a possibility of scoring a point. Any legally played ball that is resting on the court or in motion as the result of being hit by another live ball. Also, any ball still in the possession of a participant waiting to play.

measuring devices - feet, hands, fingers, twigs, string, tape measures, television antennas, or more specialized implements for determining who has the point. See Chapter 1, The Game, for details on measuring and Chapter 5, The Equipment, for information on purchasing the devices.

nearest ball rule - accepted order of play whereby the team with the ball nearest to the object ball stands aside and allows the other team to bowl until they establish the nearest ball (or they run out of balls in the attempt). The obligation to deliver the next ball always belongs to the team that is out, not in. The same team may roll two, three, even four balls in succession if they cannot outlag or knock away the other team's point while attempting to establish the in ball.

open rules - a less structured type of play unencumbered by the stringent regulations of international play. Open rules usually govern backyard play as well as a good deal of league and tournament competition. See Chapter 8, Tournament Play & Rules.

out - not closest to the pallino. "Your team's ball is in. Our team's ball is out, so it's our turn to roll."

pallino - also called the pallina, object ball, jack, pill, cue ball. A ball that is smaller than the bocce balls (generally 1 $^3/_8$ inches in diameter as opposed to 4 1/4 inches for the larger bocce balls) that is the target in the game of bocce. In a true contest of one-ups-manship, teams vie to score points by directing their balls closer to this ball than the opposition can. The pallino, bocce's bull's eye, is always of a color visibly distinct from both team's bocce balls.

pallino advantage - the favorable position of possessing control of the object ball. The team with pallino advantage gets to roll the pallino to any legal position and must also play the first bocce ball in the round. Pallino advantage is established at the beginning of the game by coin toss (or choosing up, or some other mutually agreeable method) and subsequently goes in each round to the team that scores.

pétanque - see boules above

pointing - also lagging; rolling the bocce ball in an effort to "close in" or draw near the pallino. This is a finesse shot requiring deft touch and smooth release of the ball. It is an attempt to get as close as possible to the object ball — to score a point. Sometimes this is referred to as the punto or puntata (gentle) method. If there are separate foul lines for pointing and hitting, players must use the pointing or roll line (the one closer to the end from which you are playing) for this shot. Those skilled at pointing are considered good pointers or laggers. During a postgame recap you may reflect that your team pointed very well but your shooting was off.

punto - smooth roll for point. See pointing above.

raffa (see also hitting) - a fast rolling shot intended to knock an opponent's ball away or to drive the pallino to a new position. Striking its target on the roll, this smash shot is referred to as hitting, spocking, popping, or bombing. Raffa shots usually include a two-, three- or four-step approach reminiscent of candlepin or tenpin bowling. Although a raffa in recreational play is usually rolled like a bowler trying for a strike, a true international competition raffa must be lofted beyond the raffa line, which is three meters in front of the pointing or lagging line.

round - same as frame above.

rule of advantage - the option given to a team when opponents have committed an infraction. The option is to accept the result of the illegal play or to remove the illegally delivered ball and return all balls to their original positions.

selling the point - colorful expression used when a player inadvertently gives the point to his opponent by 1) knocking his own ball out of contention, 2) bumping the opponent's ball into scoring position or 3) redirecting the pallino away from his team's ball(s) or toward the other team's ball(s). "I'm so angry at myself. I sold the point!"

sideboards - on enclosed rectangular courts, a continuous railing of 10- to 12-inch high wood planking (often pressure treated) that serves to keep the bocce balls on the alley and in play.

singles - the game of bocce played one-on-one with each player rolling four balls. Sometimes referred to as testa/testa (head to head).

spock - to hit a ball with great force to displace its position. Derived from the Italian spaccare, to break. Americanized, the term is generally used as a verb, "I'll try to spock the ball that's closest to the pallino." Players may advance to the spock line when attempting this shot (also called a hit, pop, or bomb). See hitting above.

spock line - also hitting line; on official courts, the line over which a player attempting to hit or spock may not pass until the ball has left the hand.

standing hitter - a player who attempts to hit or spock without taking an approach. Remaining stationary, the player releases a raffa or volo shot. Though they use no approach steps, these players are entitled to advance to the spock line.

swingboard - see endboards

testa/testa - see singles above.

unified - in Special Olympics a doubles game pairing Special Olympians and their Special Partners on the same team. Each team stations one Special Olympian and one Special Partner at each end of the court.

volo - an aerial shot intended to knock an opponent's ball out of scoring position or displace the pallino. Skilled players need to approach 80 to 90% success rate on these airborne knockaway attempts. Some tournament events hold shoot-outs (like the NBA three-point shoot-out) where players compete in a voloing exhibition. Target balls are placed at different locations on the court, some behind other balls adding to the difficulty, and players try to take the volo title by scoring the greatest number of hits.

winning score - bocce games may be played to any predetermined count. Winning totals of 11, 12, 15 and 16 are most common. Unlike some other sports, you don't have to win by two points. The team to first reach the agreed upon score wins the game.

Chapter 3
The Game, A Closer Look

Now that you have read about and played a little bocce, let's take a closer look at the ancient pastime. When Italian immigrants at the turn of the century landed at Ellis Island, bocce passed through customs with them. Once in America, Italians tended to keep the game to themselves, playing in backyards and at their social clubs. For many, it was a way of hanging on to the old country — a nostalgic glimpse of their native land. From the outset it was an Italian's diversion, and it was distinctively an Italian man's sport. Bocce's recent resurgence is largely due to the fact that non-Italians, young players and women have embraced the game. The increasing number of courts constructed in public parks is also promoting the sport's growth. Today, parents who want to share the game with their children don't have to spend the afternoon at the social club. They can get outside and enjoy the game and the outdoors. While Italians still seem to be the most zealous advocates of bocce (and very good players), they now share the fun with others. Anyone can play, regardless of age, strength or physical condition. If you can roll a ball about the size and weight of a candlepin bowling ball, you can play. Bocce has truly become a game for all people. Having moved slowly but steadily away from its ethnic and male dominated upbringing, bocce has reached the mainstream.

Quite similar to the French game of boules or pétanque and the English game of lawn bowls, bocce has subtle differences. Pétanque uses small metal balls that are lofted in an underhand, palm down fashion. And while some use the term bocce as a synonym for lawn bowling, the two are different games. Lawn bowls are large, biased (weighted on one side) balls which curve or hook during their path to the target. In the United States, bocce is much more widely played than lawn bowls and boules. But when grouped together, the three ball-and-target games stand with soccer and golf as the three largest participatory sports in the world.

Bocci Ball

by Frank Cappelli

How 'bout a friendly game of bocci?
We'll take our turns, we'll take our aim so nicely
We'll throw the little round poleena now
Throw the ball
The bocci ball
Please go first and toss your ball as close to the poleena as you can
Throw the ball
The bocci ball
We all watch as you show us how you play the game, mio caro amico
Your toss is smooth, we look and lean-a
The ball is going toward the small poleena
We can see it is a very good toss
Throw the ball
The bocci ball
We have heard you, now we see you, all the best to you, oh mio caro amico
Your toss is nice, we look and lean-a
The ball is going toward the small poleena
We can see it is a very good toss
Throw the ball
The bocci ball
Let us watch you as you try to get your ball slightly closer than mine
Your toss is grand, we watch and lean-a
The ball is going toward the small poleena
And we can see it is a very good toss
Throw the ball
The bocci ball
It's your turn and we all see how good at bocci ball you really, really, really are
Your toss is smooth, we look and lean-a
The ball is going toward the small poleena
We can see it is a very good toss
We walk together toward the poleena
To find who's closer and to find the winn-a
It's a tie so let us play again

Lyrics reprinted from the musical cassette tape *Pass the Coconut* with permission of F.E. Cappelli Publishing Co., 717 North Meadowcroft Ave., Pittsburg, PA 15216

Bocce's Attraction Today

Formal bocce is played on official courts of hard, compacted clay or stone dust with round, approximately two-pound, unbiased balls four to five inches in diameter. Singles, doubles, and games with foursomes are popular with very little variation in the rules. Bocce requires good judgment of distance and the ability to size up a situation and determine what type of shot or strategy is called for. An eye for analyzing the contour and rough spots or divots on a playing surface is helpful, too. Some bocce players claim that the game helps their golf, bowling, shuffleboard and horseshoes since it has features of all these games. In one way, the game is like slow-pitch softball. The slow-pitch delivery, with its six- to twelve-foot arc, is easy to hit, but not that easy to hit well. Similarly, bocce is easy to play, but not that easy to play well. "Although an easy game to learn," comments Phil Ferrari, president of the World Bocce Association, "bocce takes a lifetime to master."

Played widely in the United States both as an organized sport and as informal recreation, part of bocce's attraction is that it can be learned in minutes. Another plus for bocce is that the subtle nuances and strategies of play are endless. People learn how to play quickly, since the open rules are easily understood, but they continue learning as long as they compete. Equipment costs are minimal, and maintenance expense is virtually nonexistent, which makes bocce doubly attractive in this era of budgetary restraint. Though there exists a wide range of specialized bocce shoes, clothing and exotic measuring devices, all you really need is a set of bocce balls and a place to play. Youth and physical attributes are not essential, and games lasting 15 minutes to several hours are played indoors and out. The length of games depends on the skill of the competitors and the type of game being played (international rules played by very skillful players tend to be long games). Bocce players come in all ages and both sexes. Increasingly, the physically and mentally challenged are taking part in the game. Finally, there are very few injuries associated with bocce (okay, so you might drop a ball on your toe occasionally). Sometimes a bocce ball or pallino becomes a dangerous projectile made airborne by a volo or raffa shot. Fences around spectator areas are common and are being constructed with fine mesh to contain the pallino (especially near the ends where the greatest number of balls become missiles). It is best to watch a game from the sides or from the end of the shooter, rather than from the end toward which the balls are rolling.

Most official courts are currently located in social clubs requiring paid membership, but a movement is on to bring the game out of the private sector and into the public. To this end public outdoor courts are being constructed in many parts of the country. In addition we hear investors talk of building indoor courts and renting playing time as in a pool hall.

Recreational Bocce

Just as Italians brought different dialects to this country — so did they bring regionalized variations of the rules of bocce. A movement toward standardization is gaining momentum, but there is as yet little consistency in the rules of play from one area of the country to another. In Chapter 1 we introduced the game and what have been called open rules, a recreational style of play with very few regulations. The game can proceed unencumbered by endless restrictions for almost anything goes (more on rules in Chapter 8, Tournament Play & Rules).

As we have stated, the game can be played almost anywhere on a variety of surfaces; the backyard, a dirt road, the beach, a golf course, fair grounds or public park. Played on a reasonably level or somewhat hilly surface, the game calls for a variety of skills and strategies and produces rich variations. No two games are ever exactly alike.

The Bocce Shots — Punto, Raffa, & Volo

The playing surface and the position of previously played balls determine which type of delivery is called for. Balls may be rolled gently for point (the punto shot), rolled fast to knock another ball away (the raffa shot), or lofted in the air (volo). For all bocce shots, the ball must be released before the player oversteps the foul line. (See foul lines, Chapter 4)

The Punto Shot — Pointing

On smooth, fast surfaces, players tend to roll the ball for point, holding it with palm up or palm down. Players with very good touch like to release smoothly, palm up, letting the ball roll off the fingertips. Executed properly, this imparts a 12 o'clock to 6 o'clock rotation on the ball. This release is much like that of a pure shooter in basketball. The hooper follows through with arm extended high, rolling the ball off the fingertips, and sends the ball sailing toward the basket with good backspin. A good way to practice this fingertip-release bocce delivery is to wrap a single piece of electrical tape around the center of a ball. Grasp the ball, palm up, with the tape running north to south. Place the middle finger on the tape and one finger on each side of the tape. Position the thumb and little finger on either side of the ball for balance, and roll the ball smoothly off the fingers. Pay close attention to the tape as the ball moves along its path. Thrown properly, the ball reveals a solid black stripe, top to bottom. Any deviation in the stripe or wobbling motion indicates a faulty release (ball coming off the side of the fingers or not coming off fingers evenly).

Many good players roll for point in an entirely different manner. They grip the ball lightly (palm up or down) and toss it a few feet in front of the foul line, releasing all five fingers at once. For them, the touch is in the backswing and release. In either case a good deal of practice is needed to develop the deft release necessary for this most crucial shot in bocce. As we have seen, the game involves strategy, skill and finesse. But, above all, bocce is a game of touch.

Taping a ball is an excellent way to practice pointing.

Some Points on Pointing

The grip should be light with the palm facing the target. An alternate style is to face the back of the hand to the target. This release helps slow the ball down on fast courts due to backspin, but makes rolling the ball off the fingertips impossible. Proponents of the palm-down toss maintain that it keeps the ball on line better because the backspin tends to "dig in," preventing the ball from diverting left or right. They also feel that there is less chance for the wrist or hand to twist inadvertently during the delivery since this is a more natural position. If you let your hands hang down by your side, you will see that the palm-up release requires an almost 180-degree rotation of the forearm. Try both types of delivery. See what works best for you. The arm should be kept close to the body during the backswing. The right hander generally places the right foot forward and the lefty has the left foot forward, but this is not a hard and fast rule. Regardless, most of the body weight should be on the front foot, with the back foot on the ground for balance. Some players place one foot beside the other, and simply bend at the waist and roll. Still others start with both feet together, then deliver while taking a step forward with one foot. Of course, this makes it necessary for the player to begin a step behind the foul line, while the previous methods allow you to cozy right up to it. Some players move forward over the foul line after the ball is released, maintaining that moving directly toward the target promotes better accuracy. Indeed, in recreational play it is not uncommon to see an enthusiastic player toss his ball and run up behind and then alongside it, encouraging and coaxing it toward its destination.

Two examples of pointing styles

It is important to bend at the waist and keep the body square to the target. Maintain balance and keep the ball and hand at about the same level as the ankle. Keep the arm path straight throughout the delivery, and make a smooth follow-through. The amount of backswing is directly proportional to the distance the ball must travel. You may sight directly on the target or pick a spot out in front of the release point as some tenpin and candlepin bowlers do. Spot bowlers claim that it is much easier to hit a closer target. Selecting a target zone or drop zone instead of zeroing in on the object ball is a technique that is controversial among bocce players. Some swear by it. Others swear at it. The first group points out that golfers look at the ball, not the hole when putting and that top notch bowlers key on spots on the lane, not the pins. The other group says it's tough to hit what you're not looking at. Give both styles a go, and decide for yourself. Keeping the head down and focusing on the target (target ball or drop zone) even after releasing the ball fosters good concentration. Experiment with all the deliveries and discover what works best for you. Be advised that most of the top players in the world use the drop zone technique. Ken Dothée, president of the United States Bocce Federation reminds us that the arm and hand are on the side of the body, while the eyes are in the center. "Line up your arm with the target, not the center of your body," says Dothée. "This allows you to make a straight release and prevents the arm from crossing in front of your body during the delivery."

Suggestions for Practicing Pointing

To improve accuracy, here is a technique long used by those learning to become fast-pitch softball pitchers. The would-be pitchers first learn the proper grip and delivery, then find a wall to toss against. Initially, they just try to hit the wall anywhere, and field the carom. With success, they move to increasingly smaller targets, trying to hit inside a large chalked box, then a smaller box, and finally a square approximating the size of the strike zone. Bocce's version of this technique involves marking a large circle on your playing surface. Now roll bocce balls with the right amount of force to get them to stop within the ring. As you gain proficiency, make the circle increasingly smaller. If

Practicing with cones

you roll eight balls, it is not enough to land two or three dead center and scatter the rest outside the circle. To develop consistency is to cluster a majority of the bocce balls somewhere in the target zone every time. When you get to this point, shrink the target. It is important to spend enough time developing a high percentage of accuracy with large circles before progressing to smaller ones. Also, decrease the size of the circle by small increments rather than going directly from a large circumference to a small one.

To hone the ability to roll the ball the proper distance, mark two parallel lines across the court and practice rolling balls that come to rest anywhere within these lines. Vary the position of the parallel lines and practice, practice, practice. This drill and the previous one are more enjoyable if practiced with a partner, adding an element of competition to the activity.

To work on controlling the direction or glide path of the bocce ball, create one-foot wide lanes down the court using cones or other marking devices. Roll the ball evenly at different speeds and practice this very important phase of the game. On a level surface, your goal is to roll each ball from one end to the other without dislodging any cones.

The Raffa

The raffa is a fast rolling shot intended to knock an opponent's ball away or to direct the pallino to a new position. For example, your opponent has pallino advantage and rolls the first ball one inch from the object ball. It's probably going to be easier for you to try to hit that ball away than to roll one closer than an inch from pallino. Some bocce enthusiasts fear that the raffa's increasing popularity will discourage coed play since women's leagues tend to emphasize finesse and strategy over brute strength, but increasingly women players are employing the various hitting techniques. Donna Allen of the USBF maintains that "The key to the successful raffa shot is the follow-through. Therefore, it has been embraced by women players over the more physically demanding volo shot." The result is that women, according to Allen, "are becoming more well-rounded and competitive players."

Reminiscent of a break shot in billiards, the raffa is usually made with an approach similar to that of a tenpin or candlepin bowler. Remember, on all shots the player must release the ball before overstepping the foul line or a foot foul results. Many sets of rules mandate one foul line for pointing and a second for raffa and volo attempts. This second line, farther up the alley, allows the bocce player room for several approach steps. Many players intentionally go over the foul line after releasing the ball. Rather than stopping abruptly at the foul stripe, they prefer to improve accuracy by keeping their body's momentum going in the direction of the target. Other players take a three- or four-step delivery like in bowling, but stop at the foul line. Still others are standing hitters. They stand still, swinging only the arm, hand, and ball to unload a direct hit on the target. Be aware that on some courts the foul lines are painted on the sideboards while on others they are drawn across the surface of the court. In most informal bocce, many players overstep the foul line before releasing the ball and, though this provokes a good deal of grumbling from opponents, foot fouls are rarely called.

Raffa Technique

As in bowling, players can set their own style of stance, approach and delivery. Rolling a bocce or bowling ball presents fewer absolutes than hitting a baseball or serving a tennis ball. The key is to stay relaxed and comfortable. Some players begin by holding the ball at eye level and sighting over it. Others bend deeply at the waist, and still others hold the ball out at arm's length pointing toward the target. You can choose any style. The important thing is to use the exact same stance, approach and delivery every time. You must develop consistency in front of the foul line before you'll see consistent results down by the object ball.

Your initial distance from the foul line depends on the number and size of the steps in your approach (usually three or four). The feet are together or one is slightly ahead of the other. Keep the body square to the foul line, and practice until your steps are the same length each time. The steps should be straight (watch out for drifting left or right), slow and under control. The raffa attempt on a bocce court requires the same approach as a strike or spare attempt on the bowling alley, without the slide. If you use a three-or four-step (or five-step) approach at the bowling alley, use the same technique during raffa attempts.

In the three-step approach, the ball drops down and back for the backswing during the first step, which the right-hander takes with the left foot. On the second step the ball is almost at the top of the backswing. The third step is the slide in bowling, with shoulders square to the target and the other arm out for balance. Instead of the slide, the bocce player either stops abruptly upon release, or continues forward across the foul line *after the release* (the top players in the world continue forward after the release). The four-step approach is similar to the three-step with the additional step beginning with the right foot (for right-handers). Many players need this extra step to bring the entire stance, approach and delivery into synch. Regardless of the number of steps, they must be natural, rhythmic and well-coordinated.

Speed Versus Accuracy

There are many hard hitters in bocce, often an example of overkill. A direct hit with high velocity sends the target ball flying, but often results in a long post-impact roll for the raffa. You've displaced the opponent's close point, but your ball isn't very near to the pallino either. Of course, if you had a previously played ball(s) close to the pallino, a clean takeout of the opponent's ball brings it (them) into scoring position. If you are determined to become a hard thrower, make sure that you do not sacrifice accuracy for speed.

Key Points to Emphasize for the Raffa:

1. Bend at the waist during the approach and delivery.
2. Keep the arm swing close to the body.
3. The backswing should not be higher than shoulder level.
4. Make the approach steps in a straight line to the target.
5. The first step should be taken by the foot opposite to the throwing arm.
6. Keep the shoulders square to the target.
7. Release the ball on the last step with knees and toes pointed straight at the target.
8. Do not release too soon. Bend at the waist and extend the arm, letting go of the ball out in front of the body (but toward the side of the throwing hand eye).
9. If you prefer rolling off the fingertips, roll the ball like a bowler trying for a strike. If you prefer the loft or lob, then the farther the target the higher your release point should be. Proponents of this method claim that the farther the ball rolls, the more its chance of going off line.

The raffa technique — also referred to as hitting, spocking, popping or bombing. In international play a true raffa must be lofted beyond the raffa line which is three meters in front of the pointing line.

10. Follow-through high with a full sweep of the arm.
11. Stress accuracy over speed.
12. Keep the arm path in a straight pendulum-type swing — the arm goes down, back, forward, and to follow-through position in the same constant arc.
13. Make the elements of the stance, approach, delivery and follow-through consistent every time.
14. Emphasize concentration, which is a critical factor in increasing the percentage of hits scored.

Some Suggestions for Practicing The Raffa

Spend some time working on stance, approach and delivery with no ball. Start by assuming a comfortable starting point and stance, and walk up to the foul line concentrating on just the steps (no arm movement). Next, walk the approach and add the arm swing, delivering an imaginary ball. Now pick up the ball and go through the motion again, but do not roll the ball. Let the weight of the ball do the work of the arm swing. Finally, make a complete approach and delivery rolling at a target. Place target balls at close range for practice until you can hit 80% or better before moving the target farther away. Remember to make the approach to the launch point slow and smooth and at a constant speed. Fouling often occurs when steps are too long or too fast. Have someone watch you for foot fouls or set up a video camera perpendicular to the foul line. If you have difficulty hitting your target even at close range, try making the target larger by placing several balls in a cluster. As your percentage of hits increases, make the target increasingly smaller, then increasingly farther away. Practice, practice, practice.

The Volo Shot

Note: The suggestions listed here apply to the volo shot in backyard or recreational settings. True international volo shots must meet certain additional restrictions. See Chapter 9, International Play.

When playing on grass, rough, or soft surfaces, it is often necessary to loft the ball into the air, letting it bounce and then run up to the target. This is a form of what bocce players call a volo shot

(an aerial toss). The volo, traditionally used to knock an opponent's ball away, allows for better accuracy than rolling on rough, uneven surfaces. With practice altering the height and distance of the lob and analyzing the subsequent roll of the ball, a player can add this effective weapon to his arsenal of shots. Some players loft the ball half way or more toward the target and let it run the rest of way. The volo shot is best controlled by holding the ball palm down. Sometimes you will need to throw it with backspin to get it to stop quickly after it lands. For very long volos, you may want to toss the ball with the palm facing up to impart more forward spin thus increasing its post-landing carry. In any case, unless your lawn is very level, it is often difficult to roll for points on grass with consistent results.

A variation of this shot is good for dealing with rough surface just in front of the playing line. Simply lob the ball over the rough area and let it roll to the target. For a short lob, release the ball at about the level of the knee. The faster the surface, the higher the release point and trajectory. For high loft shots, the release point should be at the level of the upper thigh or above. The longer the toss, the more exaggerated the backswing must be. Swing the arm in a straight line with the target and push off the legs on the release. Follow-through high. Practice by placing an object on the playing surface which the ball must pass over on its way to the target.

The traditional volo shot is tossed into the air in an attempt to strike its target on the fly. A skillful player can make a neat transfer of energy shot in which his ball hits the opponent's ball, sending it flying but leaving his ball in the approximate spot that it struck. Another option is to strike the ground with the volo a foot or two before the target, and have it hit the target on the roll. After the initial impact, the volo's energy of motion is transferred to the target ball which ricochets away leaving your ball in contention.

Top bocce players use an approach similar to the raffa approach when delivering a volo. However, the stance and approach are much more upright and the ball is usually tossed with palm down, although the palm-up delivery also seems to be gaining favor. Most volo shooters use a four-step approach and continue moving past the foul line directly toward the target after they release the ball. We suggest mastering the stationary throw before progressing to this technique.

Volo Technique

Begin working on the last two steps of the four-step approach since these are the most critical. During these steps the arm swing and launch is made. Breaking down and mastering these two steps, then, is essential before advancing.

Stand at the foul line with feet together and arms by the side. Take two steps backward to bring yourself into correct position for this drill. The first step is taken with the foot opposite the throwing

Two-step approach

Four-step approach

arm. As this step is taken, bring the arm swing back in a straight pendulum-like movement. The arm should be at the top of the backswing as the second step is started. The arm comes forward to the launch point on the second step. Continue to move forward toward the target after you release the ball. This follow-through fosters better accuracy, and is not a foot foul unless you overstep the line before releasing the shot.

Once the two-step approach is mastered, advance to the four-step method. Begin four steps from the foul line with the feet together and arms by the side. Many players prefer a stance with the ball held at waist, chest or eye level. With this stance the ball is often held palm up and rotated into palm down position during the arm swing. Again, the first step should be with the foot opposite to the throwing hand. The arm does not begin the backswing on this step. The backswing begins on the second step and should not reach the top of its arc until the end of the third step. The fourth step brings the arm forward in a straight line with the target and the ball is released. During the follow-through phase, the voloist continues moving in a straight line to the target, promoting greater accuracy. Use the same suggestions for practicing raffa shots listed previously for honing your volo skills. Using two sets of bocce balls when working on the volo and raffa shots makes for a more efficient practice session (more repetitions before walking to the other end of the play area to " reload").

Compete at Your Own Level

With bocce's flexibility and simplicity there is a style and level of play for you. But we must warn you. The game grows on you and eventually you are likely to yearn to play at the next higher level. You start out playing on the backyard lawn and long for an official court. You play on the court and you want to join a league or participate in tournaments. It is inevitable. Don't fight it. The beauty of the game is that it can be enjoyed on so many different levels — from recreational play in your backyard on grass, dirt, or gravel to more structured play at the social club or outdoor courts. For some, tournament play involving singles, doubles, or four-person teams is the way to go. And tournament play ranges from the very low key to the extremely cutthroat (see Chapter 8, Tournament Play & Rules). Bocce players can even compete at the national and international level, representing their country in the Special Olympics or World Cup play. The International Olympics Committee has recently recognized bocce as a sport. This is the important first step toward its becoming an Olympic sport.

Bocce is about to explode in this country. LL Bean's summer catalog advertises bocce balls in a handsome carrying case and, yes, designer bocce shoes are in vogue. "Bocce," said one thirty-something couple, " is the yuppiest thing we do." Bocce's small but enthusiastic band of promoters

expects it to become one of the top recreational sports in the USA. A set of bocce balls will be as common a household item as a television set, compact disc or videotape player. Experiencing ever-rising popularity, indoor bocce courts are sprouting up in restaurants, lounges and sports bars in various parts of the country. You can play some friendly bocce while waiting to be served, and settle the bill over a game afterward.

The introduction of bocce in American schools is beginning to gain momentum, with young people taking to the game readily. In Wilbraham, Massachusetts, bocce buff Leonard Hickey built a gorgeous 76-foot long court on his business property. He installed spectator benches, and lights the court from dusk to dawn. Local high school students spend some evenings there and are proving to be naturals at the sport. They understand the game immediately and are rapidly developing their own bocce jargon.

"You scored the point, so you get pallino privilege — it's like having the honors in golf."

"That ball is too close to beat, so take it out!"

"Yea, it's near the sideboard, so run the rail and take 'em out!"

"Good idea, even if you miss, we have three pellets left."

Maria Colangelo, a teacher of Italian at Plainville High in Connecticut runs a bocce week that culminates with a popular bocce tournament. The tourney is open only to students in her classes, a strategy that has boosted course enrollment over the years. The students practice bocce on the lawns on campus, then play at a local Italian club where the members serve as referees. The players are permitted to speak only Italian when asking questions of the referee, and of course, the official can only respond via the romance language. Ms. Colangelo's excellent program is well covered by local media, and is typical of the response bocce will get in schools in the near future.

It is amazing that within such a simple and elegant framework of play, bocce provides such limitless variation. From backyard lawns to international competitions bocce is truly a game for all people. And in what other arena could an 80-year-old grandparent compete with an eight-year-old grandchild and be on nearly equal terms?

Photo sequence of play at the beach. The gentleman makes a good point and experiences the "Joy of Bocce."

Chapter 4
The Game As Played
On Official Courts

While lawn bocce is very exciting and serves the sporting needs of a great many people, some players feel a need to advance to the next level. Playing bocce on an official court with stone dust, clay or artificial surface brings the game to that higher plane. Bocce games played on courts generally take place in social clubs or on public courts. The play may be informal "pickup" games or structured as leagues. For league games between two social clubs, three games to a match is common, after which the hosts generally provide drinks and dinner. Increasingly, especially in areas that have no public courts, bocce lovers are building their own backyard courts (instructions in Chapter 7).

As we have stated, there is movement toward rules standardization, but so far it hasn't happened. "Official" courts are 60, 70, 80 feet and longer in different areas of the country. The court game is quite different from playing in an open park where whoever has the pallino can choose the direction to throw it. In many ways the court version of bocce is similar to the game played on lawns, but it multiplies the importance of strategy and planning moves ahead. When my family and I play lawn bocce there's no telling where the pallino will end up. Sometimes even clever strategy goes for naught. But, on our newly constructed backyard court, I know the object ball will stay somewhere within the wooden banks of the 10 x 76 foot alley. I can plan what to do with each ball accordingly. Also, playing on courts includes a new dimension of skillfully played bank shots.

Finesse is a bigger factor on courts due to the fast surface of a fine, hard packed stone dust or clay. The ball cruises along on a seemingly frictionless path. Since it travels such a distance with little energy supplied by the player, finesse and touch are critical. Players need to develop a smooth release of the ball and the soft touch of a basketball shooting guard to achieve success. In addition the raffa and volo shots can be perfected on courts because the lumps, bumps and other surface abnormalities of the lawn are eliminated.

Even when played on official courts, bocce is not a physically demanding sport. Some claim great physical benefits, but this a stretch. Sure, you're using the large muscle groups of the upper and lower body, but an aerobic workout it's not! You can burn about half a calorie for each raffa shot that you take, so after a zillion games you might lose a pound. There is no pounding on your spine and knees as in basketball, no sprinting and sliding as in baseball, and no oxygen deprivation as in tennis or racquetball. You don't have to be in shape to play bocce, though physical fitness controls the fatigue factor in any competitive sport. On the other hand, the mental and social benefits of bocce are incalculable. Competing on courts or grass fosters a healthy outlook on life. And after all, bocce meets today's health and fitness standard of favoring lifetime sports over those that you can enjoy only in your youth.

Elite players maintain that fitness is a major factor in large, double elimination tournaments. Some have competed almost around the clock, from 9:00 a.m. to midnight and beyond. Furthermore, they claim that the rapid-fire shoot-out competitions held at major bocce events are among the most physically demanding endeavors in sports. Reminiscent of the NBA's three-point shoot-out, bocce's rapid-fire drill gives players the opportunity to show off their voloing ability. Competitors run from one end of the court to the other attempting to score as many hits as possible within a five-minute time limit. As you can imagine, five minutes of continuous running and tossing bocce balls in the air can make for a very tiring exercise.

Initial Toss of Pallino

The game is more structured on the court; its rules more clearly refined, if not uniform. First off, there are rules governing the initial toss of the pallino. Again, there is no standardization of the rules, it being played differently from one area to another even within the same country (see Chapter 8 for reprints of the World Bocce Association Open Rules). Most sets of rules specify that the pallino must travel a minimum distance — usually beyond the half-court marker and a minimum distance from the end board. Besides the required distance that the pallino must settle from the players, some rules stipulate that it come to rest a minimum distance from the side walls. The International Bocce Association, based in Utica, New York, has developed a set of rules that are widely used in the East (IBA rules governed play in the 1995 Special Olympics World Games). They require the first toss of pallino reach mid-court or beyond, and settle at least four feet from the endboard and 12 inches from the sideboard. If the initial toss of pallino does not satisfy all of these requirements, the pallino is returned to the player for another attempt. Most rules give the player three attempts to successfully place the pallino, after which it goes to the other team for one attempt. If that try fails, the referee places the pallino in a legal position and play resumes. The team with pallino advantage (the one who made the three unsuccessful attempts) still tosses the first ball.

Note: In recreational play, when the pallino fails to settle within legal parameters, players often agree to speed the game up by simply moving the pallino to a legal position. For example, if the ball comes to rest eight inches from the left sideboard, they move it four inches or so to the right. If it settles three feet from the endboard, they bring it forward a foot.

Foul Lines

Official courts have foul lines that players may not step past until they release the ball. Some rules stipulate a single foul line (at each end of the court), others mandate two foul lines — one for pointing and one for hitting. The reasoning for the second foul line is that many players use a three- or four-step approach when hitting or spocking. The pointing line does not allow enough runway for this shot, so a second hitting line, closer to the target, is used. In any case the player must release the ball before passing the foul line. The first foot foul committed by each player results in a warning, and subsequent fouls carry penalties. Both the raffa and the volo players can use the hitting line as their release point. Standing hitters may position themselves right at the hitting line when attempting a raffa or volo.

Pre-Game Warm-Ups

In tournaments and some recreational play, the participants roll a frame in each direction to get acclimated to the court. During this once-up and once-back practice, players attempt the various shots (punto, raffa, volo) and look for irregularities and tendencies in the surface before actual play begins. Pay close attention to how the ball rolls at various speeds. Look for any cues that might help you play various shots during the ensuing game. Play a ball or two off the sideboard to see if the carom is as you expect. Toss a raffa off the backboard to check how much bounce back you get.

Playing the Game

Regardless of the surface on which you play bocce, the roll for point is the most important skill in the game. You may be able to survive without a raffa or volo shot, but if you cannot point, you cannot compete well in bocce. A complete player needs to be able to point *and* hit, but, just as the fastball is the king of pitches in baseball, the punto is sovereign in the kingdom of bocce.

When an opponent's point is too close to outlag, good players use the raffa or volo to try to knock it away. The ideal knockaway ball strikes its target, sends it out of contention, and then settles in for the point. Even if the hit is good but the opponent's ball is still in, at least now there should be room to close in for the score. If the shot misses its mark, however, the shooter must decide if it is worth the risk to take another knockaway shot. The percentages may be better for closing in to keep the opponent from scoring multiple points.

Some good players try to spock or hit away a ball even though it is not extremely close. They want to have one of their team's balls at the backboard in case the opponents knock the object ball there later in the game. They reason that a good hit eliminates the opponent's point, and a miss puts a ball at the backboard acting as a kind of insurance policy. Purists say that there is too much play off the side and backboards. In some areas of the country, players look for every opportunity to take the object ball to the backboard. Then they simply pound the endboard to score points. Purists don't want the game dominated by play in the end zone; they want it played in the open court where luck is less a factor and touch is the dominating skill. "These guys think the game is billiards," commented one disgruntled bocce enthusiast unhappily watching balls carom off the back and sideboards. "Some of them even make the first toss of pallino off the side board," he added. "What game are they playing?"

The following is a common scenario: Team A tosses pallino and brings its first ball several inches away from the target ball. Team B tries an unsuccessful raffa and elects to try a second knockaway shot. That one misses too, leaving two of Team B's balls at the end board. Team B, after some thought, attempts a third raffa, this time driving the pallino to the backboard. The raffa shot rolls to the endboard, too. Now, three of Team B's balls are in, even though only one of their shots was a hit. Scenarios such as these are spurring a movement to institute a rule stating that a ball that hits the backboard without first hitting a ball on the court is dead. The dead ball is removed from the court, and may not score a point. Again, purists want the rules to favor the player with skill and touch. Some bocce enthusiasts want to go as far as marking the position of the balls when the object ball is near the backboard or whenever a missed volo or raffa is likely. The player must then call his shot, and if he misses and displaces other balls, all balls may be returned to their original positions (bocce's *rule of advantage* would apply, in which case the opponents could elect to return the scattered balls to their original positions, or leave them in their new locations).

Most courts have a swingboard or bumpered board (see Chapter 7, Building a Backyard Court) at each end that serves to absorb the force of a ball hitting it. Again, this design is to keep players from using the backboard as a rebounding instrument, first rifling a raffa off the board, then watching it carom back toward the pallino. The idea is to entice players to score points by using the more skillful smooth roll.

Shot Selection

Before each shot it is a good idea to stand at the backboard and analyze the situation. Select which type of shot is appropriate for the current lay of the balls. Make a quick mental picture of the distance and layout of the previously played balls. Pause briefly to let the picture come into focus. Now form a mental image of the successful completion of the shot you will attempt. Finally, block everything else out of your mind — the score, the fans, the opponents — and execute.

The smooth roll for point is the most common shot in bocce. Most players use it and one of the two knockaway shots (raffa or volo) in their game. Currently, there are very few bocce players using the volo technique here on the East Coast. You should try to master both the raffa and volo technique. Both are a bit awkward at first, but with practice they can become successful parts of your game. I was very fortunate to spend some time with Phil Ferrari, the 1993 Bocce World Singles Champ and president of the World Bocce Association, while we officiated bocce at the 1995 Special Olympics World Games. We played a lot of bocce in our spare time, and when he first introduced me to the correct raffa and volo styles, I resisted. I wasn't comfortable. "Why use a bowling-type approach?" I thought. "You can't slide on a bocce alley." And overstepping the foul line after releasing the ball didn't sit well with me either. But, after I built my own backyard court and practiced proper technique, the shots became natural and welcome additions to my game.

Thinking Ahead

Before choosing the type of shot to attempt, think ahead about the consequences of the shot. If I roll a ball here, what will my opponent likely do? Do I want to stay short of the target so as not to nudge the pallino toward an opponent's ball? Or do I want to be long so that I might push the pallino

toward my own team's previously played ball(s). When I introduced my friend, Walter Pare, to bocce, he called the game lawn chess. "You can think ahead and know the move you want to make" says Pare, "but you can't always place the pieces exactly where you want them."

Playing Bank Shots

One of the neat things about playing on an official court is the opportunity to deftly execute bank shots. I tend to agree with the purists who want to keep the game in the open court, away from the side and endboards. Nevertheless, a well-placed shot that caroms off the sideboard and slips in between two other balls and steals the point is one of the nicest feelings that bocce has to offer. (Note that some rules prohibit play off the side and endboards.) Bank shots are mastered by experimenting. Practice hitting the boards at different angles and different speeds. Watch the carom and make a mental file of the results. Teach yourself this effective technique and add it to your game.

Moving the Pallino to Gain Advantage

Be aware that the position of the pallino may change at any time during a frame. A well-placed raffa or volo attempt can save the day by redirecting the pallino away from one team's balls and toward the other's. Keep this in mind during play. Consider where your opponent may try to move the pallino to gain an advantage, and how you can minimize the chance of this happening. Often, this simply means keeping a ball near the endboard to prevent the other team from scoring easy points by bringing the object ball there.

Courting Bocce & More Courts

Bocce may be the sleeping giant of sports. For it to really explode in America many more courts need to be constructed. The sport needs more visibility, more exposure. Promoters are looking for media coverage and corporate support for big time tournament action. They are also trying to introduce bocce into the school systems, but, while permanent courts are being installed in high schools in the Midwest and West, this is being greeted with mixed results. This is reminiscent of the introduction of soccer into American schools. Officials were skeptical at first, but soccer flourishes today because people realized how inexpensive and easy it was to initiate soccer programs. The same is true for bocce.

According to demographic research done by the United States Bocce Federation, the average age of the American bocce player has decreased by almost 20 years since the 1980s (when it was age 60). The visibility of the game has increased dramatically due to the construction of outdoor facilities. Bocce is especially popular in California and Florida where residents play outdoors year-round. Some employers are even building courts on job sites, creating a pleasant diversion for hard-working people. Installing signs that summarize the rules and give a little history of the game serves to prevent vandalism and misuse of the alleys (in one California park, visitors used the bocce courts as horseshoe pits). Bocce promoters hope to get bocce courts in schools, park and recreation departments, senior centers, youth clubs, new housing developments, hospitals, and even correctional facilities. While seeking corporate and business sponsorships, the ultimate goal is to increase tournament exposure and lure the television market.

For the sport to continue its growth, it must have standardization of equipment and courts. Today bowling balls, pins and alleys are uniform across the country. There is no reason the same consistency can't be true of bocce.

Bocce Etiquette

1. Don't take too long thinking over a shot.
2. Don't over-coach or tell teammates what to do on each shot. To execute well, a player needs to take the shot that he feels comfortable with.
3. Don't wander off — stay with the team even when you have completed delivery of your allotted bocce balls.
4. Be ready to play when it's your turn.
5. Stay under emotional control at all times.
6. Remain quiet while others take their turn.
7. After each frame, leave balls in place until the referee officially awards points.
8. Losing team buys the drinks.

Chapter 5
The Equipment

One of the nifty things about bocce is that you need very little equipment to enjoy the game. All you require is a set of bocce balls that, with proper care, can last a lifetime. Sure, there are designer shoes and apparel and exotic measuring devices, but these are extras. My family and friends played backyard recreational bocce for years with nothing more than a good set of bocce balls. We didn't even own a fancy measuring device. The points that we couldn't call by eye we measured with our feet, hands, twigs, string, an old car antenna or a tape measure. For many of us, though, bocce becomes an addiction. We want to read and learn more about it, practice and play more often, and explore bocce related paraphernalia. What follows is a brief primer on the equipment, the publications, and their distributors. There are some pretty neat gadgets and bocce gear that make terrific gifts for the bocce buff in your life.

Bocce Balls

First off, don't buy an inferior set just to save a few dollars. The balls may be the only bocce-related purchase you'll ever make, so it should be a cost-effective one. A good quality set will cost you $60 to $100 or more and may include a warranty of up to five years. Bocce balls are commonly $4 \frac{1}{4}$ inches in diameter and weigh about two pounds, with specifications varying slightly from one manufacturer to another (metric equivalents are 100 to 120 mm and 900 to 1100 grams). The pallino is approximately $2 \frac{1}{8}$ inches (55-60 mm) in diameter, but some sets come with a smaller $1 \frac{1}{2}$ inch (36-41 mm) object ball. Most dealers package a set of eight balls and a pallino. This usually includes four balls of one color, four of another color, and a pallino of a third color. Bocce balls traditionally were made of wood, but today most are of composition material much like bowling balls (some international play mandates metal balls). Some sets further distinguish the four balls of each color with engraved marks to tell one teammate's balls from another. This is of dubious advantage since telling which teammate threw which ball is not nearly as important as telling which team's ball is which. If you are going to play exclusively on grass, try to avoid the smaller object balls. Small pallinos tend to be obscured even by closely cropped lawns. My family has used a croquet ball as the object ball when playing on grass, and the official bocce pallino when we're on the alley. Some manufacturers include a carrying case with the set of balls, others make it an extra. Careful — some of the more expensive European balls come four to a set instead of eight and don't include a pallino (and metal balls are sold in sets of two). These are favored by the extremely competitive players who bring their personal bocce balls to every match. These players want the consistency that using the same bocce balls every game brings. They also tend to carry a cloth or chamois to wipe dust and debris from the ball before each toss.

A set of bocce balls

Bocce Ball Dealers

Many U.S. sporting goods manufacturers offer bocce sets for sale. Following is a brief list of dealers who specialize in bocce and outdoor sports equipment. If available, we have included ball specifications. You can also try the sporting goods departments of stores like Bradlee's, K-Mart, and Caldor, but be advised that the popularity of bocce in your area will have an impact on the store's inventory. Recently, we conducted a telephone survey in northeastern Massachusetts to determine which department stores stocked bocce equipment. More than a few of those answering the phones had never heard of bocce, and connected us with the gas grilles and camping department to talk about hibachis.

General Sportcraft Co. Ltd., 140 Woodbine St., Bergenfield, NJ 07621. Phone: (201) 384-4242, Telefax (201) 387-8128.

General Sportcraft offers several sets of composition and wood balls in boxed carrying cases. Zippered bocce bag is an extra. *The Champion Series* (109 mm composition balls, 60 mm pallino) is "designed for tournament player's competitive requirements." *The Contender Series* (two different sets - 110 mm wood balls with 55 mm pallino, and 100 mm wood balls with 41 mm pallino) is designed "to the standards of the accomplished competitive player." Finally, General Sportcraft offers two different sets in their *Classic Series*. One set features 90 mm balls and the other 4 inches. Both are for "family and recreational play."

Hutch Sports USA Inc., 1835 Airport Exchange Blvd., Suite 100, Erlanger, KY 41018. Phone: 1-800-727-4511, (606) 282-9000, Fax: (606) 282-7308. Hutch offers several sets of eight balls and a pallino that were formerly Forster products. The World Cup set of phenolic composition is their top-of-the-line product. It includes four blue and four white balls 110 mm (4 $^{11}/_{32}$") in diameter, and a 57 mm (2 $^1/_4$") pallino. The set comes with a distance measuring device, a durable nylon carry bag, rules (International Bocce Association), instructions and warranty information.

Hutch also sells a green and red Tournament Set (phenolic composition) with the same size specifications as above. This set features custom-etched patterns to differentiate one teammate's balls from another's. Includes measuring device, carry bag, rules, instructions and warranty information.

Hutch's Competitors Set is comprised of eight 100 mm (4") compressed wood balls, a 36 mm (1 $^1/_2$") wood pallino, a measuring device, rules, instructions and warranty information. Hutch also offers a similar polymer set formerly distributed by MacGregor that includes a measuring device, rules and instructions.

International Bocce Association, Inc., 187 Proctor Boulevard, Utica, NY 13501. Phone: (315) 733-9611. The IBA sells a 109 mm set of eight (four red, four green) synthetic phenolic resin balls, a pallino, and a rulebook. IBA also stocks replacement balls and pallinos.

Regent Sports Corp., 45 Ranick Road, Hauppauge, NY 11787. Phone: (516) 234-2800.

Regent markets most of their Italian-made bocce line under the Halex name. The *90010 International Series* includes eight 90 mm (3 $^5/_8$") diameter wood composition balls with acrylic finish. There are two red, two blue, two green and two yellow balls; one 40 mm (1 $^5/_8$") diameter yellow jack; and complete rules and instructions including court layout. The *90020 International Series* is the same as above except that the eight balls are 100 mm (4") in diameter. The *90030 Professional Series* includes eight 110 mm (4 $^3/_8$") diameter phenolic balls, four red and four green balls (each color with two scoring patterns), on 50 mm (2") diameter yellow jack, and complete rules and instructions including court layout.

Professional Series 90030

Still under the Regent name is an inexpensive set of plastic, colorful water-filled bocce balls. Included are 100 mm balls — two red, two blue, two green, two yellow and one white 40 mm object ball. The small, lightweight, eye-catching balls are ideal for children.

United States Bocce Federation (USBF), President Ken Dothée, 920 Harbor View Drive, Martinez, CA 94553-2762. Phone: (510) 229-2157, Fax: (510) 370-6986. The distributor for

Regent's colorful children's set

the USBF is Bocce - Sport U.S.A., 920 Harbor View Drive, Martinez, CA 94553. Telephone: (510) 229-2157, Fax: 510-370-6986.

Bocce - Sport U.S.A.'s *American Championship Bocce Set* consists of four blue and white (107 mm, 920 gram) balls, four red and white balls, a red pallino, and rules. A variety of tote bags for two, four or eight balls (all with extra compartments) are available at an extra cost. Bocce - Sports U.S.A. also carries a line of metal balls for both lagging and shooting (including a special ball designed to minimize the bounce). Also in stock are replacement balls and pallinos. USBF members are entitled to a 10% discount on all purchases.

Wonderful World Of Bocce Association (WWOBA), President Rico Daniele, 899 Main Street Springfield, MA 01103. Phone: 1-800-BOCCE 54 (1-800-262-2354), Fax: (413) 732-8941.

WWOBA carries several different sets of balls, including bocce sets made in Italy, as well as a large line of bocce-related products.

World Bocce Association, 1098 West Irving Park Road, Bensenville, IL 60106, President Phil Ferrari, Phone: (708) 860-2623, 1-800 OK-BOCCE, Fax: (708) 595-2541.

A Word About Playing Rules That Accompany Your Purchase

There are different sets of rules that govern bocce play in America. The only rules that are standardized are the true international rules discussed in Chapter 9. Any set of rules that comes with your purchase should be taken for what it is — a set of rules. For example, International Bocce Association rules accompany many sets of balls. IBA rules, established in 1980, are very thorough. They are used in many tournaments in the East and were even adopted for the 1995 Special Olympics World Games in West Haven, Connecticut. The IBA mandates a 60 x 12 foot court (short by many other groups' standards). The point is that these are one group's "official" specifications for the game. There are others. Consider our Chapters 7 and 8 before accepting any group's court layout or playing rules as law.

Measuring Devices

In informal recreational bocce, you can get by without a formal measuring device, using hands, feet, string, twigs, car antenna, or other household objects to determine points. Most families have a tape measure in the garage or workshop, and that works very well, especially for long measurements. We recommend metric measurements over English. When comparing very similar lengths, counting centimeters is much easier than calculating eighths and sixteenths of an inch. The ever-ready tape measure is a staple at most spirited bocce games. Often, the sport produces something akin to a football huddle — a crowd engulfing the object ball anxiously awaiting the results of a measurement.

There are many measuring devices specifically designed for the ball-and-target games of bocce, boules and lawn bowls. Following are some that we tested and like.

Bocce - Sport U.S.A., Hutch Sports USA, the World Bocce Association, and WWOBA all stock a wonderful measuring implement called the Kenselite Telescopic Bowls Measure. It is a small metal telescopic device not much bigger than a ball point pen (approximately six inches when closed). The ingeniously devised tool is for inside measurement. The player or referee first estimates the distance between the pallino and the two bocce balls to be compared. Then, he extends the appropriate telescopic sections to a length slightly less than that estimate. Next, he places the device between the pallino and one of the balls in question and extends it until it touches both balls. The head of the tool is equipped with a screw-top mechanism. Turning the top in one direction lengthens the tool, while winding in the opposite direction shortens it. This fine-tuning makes for very precise measuring. Finally, the measurer places the device between the pallino and the other ball and compares.

The Kenselite Telescopic Bowls Measure

This clever French measuring device has a scoring mechanism.

Like a ball point pen, The Kenselite Bowls Measure has a clasp for fastening onto your shirt pocket. Fully extended, it is one meter (approximately 39 inches) long, so you'll still need a metric tape for longer measures. For measurements less than the length of the tool, it has calipers that fold out of the way when not needed. These calipers are capable of measuring $^1/_8$ inch to 6 inches.

WWOBA and Bocce - Sports U.S.A. carry another extremely ingenious measuring implement made in France (see photo). First off, it is a small, slender metric tape measure that extends to two meters (more than six feet). The tape automatically holds its position when extended, and to retract it you have to press the green button on top. "Avoid a strong return" is printed on this in several languages, warning against fouling the internal rewinding mechanism. A thin metal post extends about a centimeter from the back end of the measure. When measuring, the end of this post is placed

Several different measuring devices are available.

against the pallino. To use this device, place it on the ground between the pallino and the ball in question. Place the rear post against the pallino and extend the tape until it touches the bocce ball. The tape will remain extended to this length. Move over to the other bocce ball in contention, and compare. Like the Kenselite product above, this measure has calipers for evaluating shorter lengths. The calipers extend from the base of the measure and fold neatly out of the way when not in use. Also tucked away in the base is a retractable point about a centimeter long used for marking the position of balls. And if all of this is not enough for you, the implement will even keep score. On one side, it has a clever spinning wheel arrangement that tracks two team's scores up to 21.

Another excellent and easy-to-obtain measuring device is the standard folding carpenter's rule. Available at any hardware store in 6' and 8' lengths, look for the rule that includes the 6" sliding metallic extension. This sliding extension makes the tool ideal for bocce measurements. Unfold the rule to a length that fits between the two balls. Now place the rule on the ground with the back end touching the pallino, and slide the extension forward until it touches the ball being measured. Carefully lift the rule, and reposition it to compare the other ball in contention.

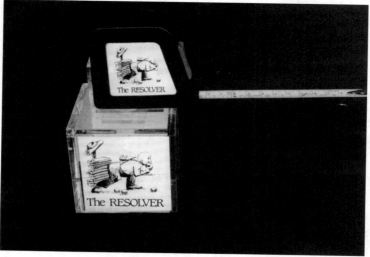

The Resolver is another method of solving bocce disputes.

Finally, a measure that deserves mention is *The Resolver*, cleverly designed by Mike Paccione of Cresskill, New Jersey. *The Resolver* is a tape measure set atop a clear acrylic cube that fits over the pallino. The tape (metric and English units) swivels 360 degrees and extends over two meters. The instructions that come with the device tell you to "extend the tape to one of the large balls in dispute and lock it by pressing the bottom of the red power lock. Swivel the extended tape to the other ball(s) in dispute. If the tape does not reach the other ball(s), then the first ball is nearest the pallino. If it touches any other ball, then it is nearest. (Use of the measuring scale on top is optional.)" Direct inquiries to *The Resolver*, P.O. Box 36, Cresskill, NJ 07626.

While all of the measures described above are excellent values, you will probably still want a conventional tape measure for determining points that are longer that a meter or two from the pallino. And take heart, soon I'm sure there will be a low frequency laser activated bocce measure.

Publications

There are five internationally acclaimed bocce publications: *United States Bocce*, *Bocce Bowls* (Australia), *Sport-Boule* (France), *Sportbocce* (Italy), and *La Suisse Bouliste* (Switzerland). United States Bocce Federation magazine editor Donna Allen claims a readership of more than 10,000 — double from five years ago. The quarterly publication includes information on the bocce scene. It features playing tips, tournament dates, and other valuable information. United States Bocce communicates with boules, pétanque, and lawn bowling groups worldwide and their U.S. Bocce Federation is recognized by the United States Amateur Athletic Union (A.A.U.), the Fédération International de Boules, and the Confederazione Boccistica Internationale. California based, the publication has a decided West Coast bent, but lists bocce happenings around the country and the world. Editor Donna Allen is as fine a spokesperson for bocce as you'll find, and is always eager to help novices with their bocce-related concerns.

Rolling Generation is the World Bocce Association's quarterly publication. President Philip Ferrari's magazine presents feature stories on bocce and its players. In Ferrari's regular column, "Rolling Pro," one of the most knowledgeable players in the country shares playing tips. Ferrari, another bocce aficionado who is ever ready to assist callers, is a strong supporter of the Special Olympics and bocce advisor to the National Italian American Foundation. Always promoting bocce, he lectures and performs demonstrations and runs charity fundraisers using the sport as the main event.

Other Paraphernalia

One of the big promoters of bocce on the East Coast, Rico Daniele of WWOBA sells bocce balls, measuring devices, other bocce related items and a line of sportswear bearing his striking bocce logo. WWOBA's full-color product catalog includes bocce scoreboards, mugs, travel bags, and a mini bocce table game played with marbles. (See photos next page) Daniele's self-published *Bocce, A Sport For Everyone*, includes everything from lists of upcoming bocce stars to recipes like pallino meatballs and fettucine a la bocce. In an effort to involve school children, Daniele has created a set of bocce cartoon character prints that relate to the nine planets of our solar system.

Phil Ferrari of the World Bocce Association (address and phone on page 42) has a product line including mugs, key chains, rings, T-shirts and sweatshirts, rule books, measuring devices, and a short promotional bocce videotape.

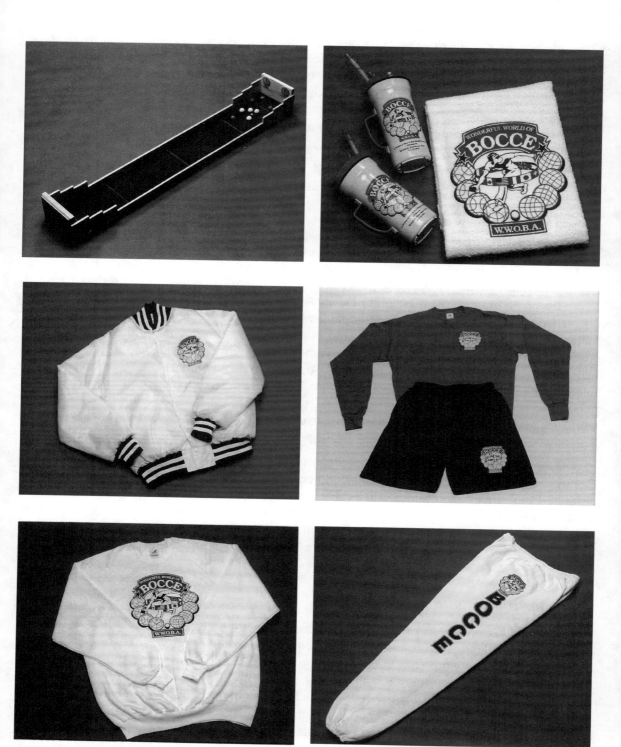

Bocce products from the WWOBA

Bocce - Sport USA (address and phone on page 42) sells bocce balls, tote bags, measuring devices, rule books and what they call bocce-abilia. These include embroidered patches, pins, key chains, and bumper strips. Affiliated with The United States Bocce Federation, members receive 10% off all purchases.

International Bocce Association, Inc., 187 Proctor Boulevard, Utica, NY 13501. Phone: (315) 733-9611.

Established in 1980, the IBA sells bocce court construction plans, measuring devices, trophies, t-shirts, caps, iron-on decals and other novelty items.

Books

The only books devoted solely to bocce that we could locate in print today are Rico Daniele's self-published work listed on page 45, and the one you are holding in your hands. I attribute this dearth of bocce books to the fact that acquisition editors have no vision...maybe they should be umpires.

Various types of bocce balls used in the last 150 years (photo courtesy of the United States Bocce Federation).

Chapter 6
Strategy & Tactics

Someone once described bocce as "a game where you throw large balls toward a smaller target ball." To me, that's like saying a fine, aged wine is just some old grapes. Bocce involves skill, finesse, strategy, a plan of attack and the ability to adjust that plan during play. The nuances of play raise it a level above those games that require only physical skills to be successful.

Some of the strategy discussed in this chapter is better suited for play on enclosed courts, and other applies more to open area play. The more experience you have playing on different courts and surfaces, the better instincts you will develop for employing the appropriate tactics. Become a student of the game by observing the play of teammates and opponents, especially cagey veterans. If you get "burned" by a particular strategy, file the data in your memory for future reference. Perhaps you can use it to "toast" an opponent sometime down the line. Above all, don't allow yourself to get beat by the same tactics in the future.

Pre-Game Strategy

In most tournament play, the participants play two mock frames (one in each direction) before each game begins. This allows the players to get a feel for the surface, and to gauge how the ball is likely to break in one direction or another. Phil Ferrari, of the World Bocce Association, suggests testing the rolling pattern of a court in the following manner. Divide the length of the court in thirds — an imaginary line four feet from each sideboard will create three narrow lanes on a 12-foot wide court. For wider or narrower courts, move your imaginary lines accordingly. Roll as many balls as you are allowed pregame on all the courts on which you will compete, and watch the glide path. Roll some balls with sufficient speed to make them reach or approach the endboard, and make note of any break in the balls' glide path. Remember that a slow moving ball will be more susceptible to this break than a fast moving one. Roll some at different speeds in each of the lanes and note the results. Test out a few bank shots and observe the angle at which the ball comes off the board. Try a few raffa (fast moving) and volo (aerial) shots, if they are in your repertoire (and permitted in the event). Get a feel for the alley and determine what form you are in. Make adjustments.

As a longtime coach, I am amazed by the number of otherwise intelligent athletes who fail to monitor their game-time performance and make adjustments. As a youth, I played basketball with an exceptional scholar-athlete who possessed a feathery-soft shooting touch. Though he was multi-talented and very bright (combined 1400+ SAT scores), he sometimes failed to make critical adjustments. During one game in which he bounced his first half-dozen shots off the front rim, our coach (who probably scored 1000 points less on his SATs) called time out and made a suggestion. "When your shots fall short," he offered, "shoot harder. Try sighting on the back rim." The hooper knocked down most of the rest of his shots, and we went on to win the ball game.

Do all of this practice and adjustment-making on all of your lanes and repeat the procedure from the opposite end of the alley. You may want to record your findings in a small notebook. For future reference, you might keep a log book of all the places you play, but be aware that grooming changes will affect the play of the alley. Use this pregame technique every time you play on an alley to see if the ball reacts as it did the last time you played there. Some people speak of a court having its own personality and, while home court advantage is a controversial notion in some sports, it's for real in bocce. In social club league games the more talented team generally wins, but the short odds are often on the host team.

The Lineup Card

A good player needs to be skilled in all phases of the game. Every player on the team must be able to point and hit. A player can't be a specialist, competent in only one area. Nevertheless, what follows is our suggestion for filling out your team's lineup card.

In a four-person team, the leadoff player is usually selected for his pointing ability. He or she is the one with the best touch. Some refer to a good point man or woman as a six-incher, implying that no matter where the pallino, he will roll a ball six inches or closer to it. For most of us this is simply wishful thinking. A player able to regularly roll a ball even 12 inches from the pallino is *very* skilled.

The number two player is generally chosen for raffa or volo ability. This player can knock away an opponent's point that is too difficult to outlag (or strike the pallino, sending it to a position more advantageous to his team). The fast rolling ball (raffa) or aerial delivery (volo) is this player's forte. The number three player is selected for versatility. This player may be called upon to point, or knock away an opponent's ball or the pallino. Finally, the number four player is the captain. He or she is generally skilled in all shots, has leadership qualities and the people skills not only to set strategy with teammates, but to act as spokesperson in dealings with tournament officials.

Shot Selection

The key in higher levels of bocce competition is not only mastering the techniques of punto, raffa and volo, but knowing when to use each. When the opponents' shot settles in for a good point, sometimes it is better to try to outlag it, while at other times a knockaway shot is in order. Of course, we have to clarify what we mean by a good point. One foot away (or less) from the pallino is a good point. So is two feet away. A ball two feet in front of the pallino can be a very good point — much better than a ball two feet to the side. A shot even three or four feet away that is in front is always a good point. The other thing to consider when deciding on hitting or pointing is the skill of the player. How good is he at hitting vs. pointing? Think ahead in all situations, asking yourself "What is likely to happen if my shot is successful?" and "What might happen if I miss?" A big factor in the choice of shots is how many balls the other team still has to play. And always bear in mind that any ball, your own or your opponent's, may change the pallino's position. Theoretically, an eight point swing could occur. Four points for their team could become four for your team with one skillful (or lucky) redirection of the object ball.

Court Surface

The court surface can come into play when deciding strategy and what type of shot to attempt. The kind of surface and its state of grooming need to be considered. Recently groomed courts tend to be faster than those that have been played on for a while. How hard or soft the surface is will affect a volo shot that lands short of its target. Rather than hit and then roll into its target, it may bounce right over it. This may lead you to select the raffa over the aerial knockaway shot.

Placing the Pallino

One of the crucial strategies in bocce is intelligent placement of the pallino. Having "pallino advantage" gives you the opportunity to go to your team's strengths or to attack your opponents' weaknesses. Of course, a big key is knowing your strong points and their weaknesses. After a few frames, a clever tactical player knows his opponents' weak spots and tries to deliver the pallino there. Rather than pitch or toss the pallino out on the fly, roll it smoothly as if you were pointing. Watch its glide path. Read its motions left or right. Use this information on your following roll(s).

If you are partial to bank shots, you may want to aim the pallino close to a sideboard. But be aware that a point that is close to pallino, but up against the sideboard, is a relatively easy target. A smart player will make a nice transfer of energy shot, hitting your ball away and leaving his in its place. If your opponents are expert at bank shots, you may want to place the object ball in the open court where they will not attempt rebound shots. The problem with spending too much time perfecting bank shots is that when you travel to other courts, the boards don't always respond predictably.

The First Roll — Initial Point

While accurate hitting is extremely important, and versatility a necessity, rolling for point is the critical skill in bocce. After all, the game evolved from the basic contest of two people trying to outdo each other tossing balls toward a target. If there were a big league bocce draft, great pointers would go in the first round. A player whose shots consistently cozy up to the pallino is in very high demand.

On the first roll establishing the initial point, you have been very successful if it takes your opponent two balls to beat it. If it takes the opposition three or four balls to outlag or knock your ball out of contention, you have been extremely successful, and your team should win the frame. The more balls your opponent uses in his attempt to outdo your initial roll, the better your chance of taking the last shot of the frame. Many players consider the first and second rolls the most critical ones since they will have an impact on who will play the last ball. When you get the last shot (the hammer, as shuffleboard players call it), you have an opportunity to win the frame. Big time college basketball coaches preach the philosophy of working hard to stay in the game so that in the final seconds, their team has a chance to win. That's the goal — to have the opportunity to win the game, even if it is with the last possession. Forcing your opponent to use several balls to beat your initial roll increases your chance of having the hammer. Possessing the hammer gives you the opportunity to win.

Some players like to leave the initial point a tad short rather than long, hoping the opponent may inadvertently bump the ball even closer. At any rate, for pointing we recommend the smooth release generating the 12 o'clock to 6 o'clock rotation that we discussed in Chapter 3. Make it your goal to place your initial point so close to pallino that your opponent needs two, three, or even four balls to beat it.

Subsequent Rolls

"Go to school" on all subsequent rolls by you, your teammates or your opponents. Don't wander off, physically or mentally. Don't think about your next shot. Pay attention and read the path of the shots that every player takes in your game. Does a ball fall in a certain direction? How does a player adjust to a bad roll? Does the adjustment work? Does the player hit the sideboard too early or too late on a bank shot? Where do players stand when making a delivery — what angles do they get? Is the angle advantageous, or would another approach be better?

Moving the Pallino to Gain Advantage

There is a version of bocce that uses a large washer as the target. The object of the game is the same — score points by directing balls closer to the target than your opponent can. The difference, of course, is that the target will remain stationary. Its place at the start of a frame will be its position at the end of the frame. But in more conventional bocce using a pallino as the target, attempting to relocate the target ball adds another dimension of strategy. Since the position of the pallino may change at any time during a frame, players need to stay mindful of this. This should be both an offensive and defensive mindset. You need to consider "Where can I redirect the pallino to gain advantage?" and "Where might my opponent try to send the pallino, and how can I prevent or minimize my disadvantage?" As we have stated earlier, often this simply means keeping a ball near the endboard to prevent the other team from scoring easy points by knocking the object ball there.

Reading the Green

In the same area of the alley, if a rolling ball falls or breaks to the left from one end, chances are it will fall to the right from the other end. A good player needs to accurately read this break and make adjustments.

When a ball falls or breaks in one direction, players tend to compensate for the break on subsequent shots. Instead of aiming at the target, they sight on a spot that, provided they get the same amount of break, will bring their ball into scoring position. This may or may not be successful. The court surface may crown or peak, and compensating by changing your aim on the next ball may surprise you. You may find it breaking in the opposite direction because it fell off the other side of the crown. For example, you take a smooth roll for point but the ball breaks twelve inches to the right preventing you from closing in for the point. You aim your next shot twelve inches farther to the left, hoping to curve this ball in to the pallino. To your surprise, this time the ball falls off to the left, still leaving your opponent with the nearest ball. When a ball's glide path is near the crown of a court surface, the direction of fall might be unpredictable. The best strategy: when a ball falls in one direction, players must adjust their position on the foul line. Move in the direction that the ball falls. Use the same glide path as on the previous shot, changing only your initial delivery point. If the ball falls right, move your body a step or two to the right. If it falls left, move to the left. This is the safest, most consistent strategy. The alternative, staying in the same position but changing the ball's path, can be effective if you have *court knowledge* (experience on the court's surface).

Taking a Chance vs. Playing it Safe

There is an element of risk in many shots that you take in a bocce game. For example, if you attempt a raffa and hit your own ball by mistake, you may help your opponent. If you play it safe, and try to outlag your opponent's ball, you may not score, but you minimize the damage. Which is the better option? That is a great question, and one for which I have a great answer. It depends. A player needs to take into consideration a host of factors. The score and the situation are critical to making a sound decision on strategy. When you are ahead and cruising toward a sure victory, you tend to get aggressive and "go for it." Behind in the score, and hoping to sneak back into the game might call for a more conservative approach. Late in the game consider — if successful, will this one daring play win the game? Has your opponent been surging in the last few frames? If the game goes to another frame, is the other team likely to take the victory? In the end trust your instincts, make the play and, successful or not, don't second guess yourself. Trust that you made an intelligent decision based on the evidence you had at the time. There always seem to be contradictory opinions on any piece of bocce strategy. It has taken me a long time, but I have finally discovered how to best evaluate the effectiveness of strategy. Wait until after the shot is taken — if it worked, it was good strategy, otherwise it was bad.

Don't be like our Massachusetts drivers who drive the same way no matter what the road conditions. Every weekday morning that we get some winter snow or slippery road conditions, there are commuters in fender benders all the way to Boston. Drive more cautiously when the conditions warrant it. Play more aggressively when conditions are right, and more cautiously when the situation calls for it. Don't end up road kill on the bocce court.

Selling the Point

Sometimes a shot doesn't turn out the way a player intended. Instead of coming in for a point, the shot bumps an opponent's ball into scoring position, or knocks his own team's point out of contention. It may even move the pallino toward the opponents' ball(s) giving him the point(s). This is selling the point, a colorful phrase that depicts one of the most disheartening happenings in the game of bocce. If you play enough, it will happen to you. Deal with it.

Taking a Stand

One kind of tactical bocce is often overlooked. Players often give little thought to selecting the best starting position for an approach or delivery. A 10- or 12-foot alley gives you a lot of options. You can legally start your approach anywhere along that 10- or 12-foot width. Walk along that line and check out the view. How much of the pallino do you see from different positions? Play the shot in your mind from the different angles and select the position that gives you the best percentage of being successful. Imagine that the shot ends up exactly as you hope it will. What will your opponents' options be then? Think ahead, then execute.

Sometimes moving to one side of the foul line or another opens up the target zone. For example, in some cases it might be advantageous to knock away your opponent's ball or the pallino. Since you aren't too concerned with which one you hit, move along the foul line to find the launch site that affords you the widest target zone. Whenever you are considering hitting, take into consideration the positions of any balls around your target. What is likely to happen if your shot is off and it hits one of them? Is this a good or bad risk to take?

In this spock attempt, the player moves well over to his right to get the best angle.

Tactical Bocce — Blocking

Many players like to close off the opponents' angle by leaving a ball short of the pallino, or strategically placing a ball to make their attempt more difficult. This concept of blocking an opponent is really playing defense. "Put some pants on it," say shuffleboard players, encouraging a teammate to place a protective block on a well-positioned point. Sometimes a block is used to concede a point, while preventing the opposition from scoring multiple points. Often, players opt for laying their last ball in front. It blocks. It defends. It has nuisance value. It gives the opposition something to think about, and often limits their options.

A good defensive mindset is to concentrate on never allowing your opponents to score more than one or two points in a frame. A big score by the opposition boosts their confidence and puts added pressure on your team. Stay in the game by avoiding giving up three- and four-point rounds.

Hit Early, Point Late

If you are debating whether to close in for point or hit your opponent's ball away, consider the following. If you are going to hit, do it first. Your point attempt might be short, and could possibly block your path to the target. Like billiards, you want to "see" the object in order to hit it. So hit early, point late. If you miss with the raffa or volo attempt, you can then decide to close in or try another hit. Teams may try to hit twice in a row, but usually not three times. If it is 11 o'clock (one point away from defeat in a twelve-point game), a team may try a third consecutive knockaway shot to save the game.

Many good players like to hit an opponent's ball away, even if it isn't extremely close. As we pointed out in Chapter 4, players want to have a ball near the backboard as a kind of insurance against the pallino being knocked there later in the game. So, the knockaway shot presents a win-win situation. It serves its team well either by hitting its target, or rolling to the backboard.

When your team has three balls to play and your opponent has but one, hitting is a good option. For example, you establish the initial point with a roll 10 inches from the object ball. Your opponents try to hit your ball away and miss. They attempt to hit again and miss. Next they point and close in to eight inches from the pallino. They have one ball left, you have three. Since they are in, it is your turn. Hitting is the right play in this situation, even if you feel you can close in, because you want their ball out of there. If it stays, it's going to be a nuisance, perhaps even preventing you from scoring big. If you miss, you still have two balls to try to close in for point or hit (you make the call!).

Not Only What, But Who?

An important strategical consideration is not only what strategy to attempt, but which player should execute the task. You might consider who is more skilled at the particular type of shot, and who feels more confident about getting the job done. Another consideration is how many balls are left for each player to roll. For example, your team has three balls left to play, the other team has none. Your opponents are in for one point. You decide to hit. One player on your team has two balls to roll, and the other has one. The player with one ball left should make the hitting attempt. If he misses, his partner will still have two chances to close in for point. If he is short or long on the first attempt, he can adjust with the second ball and should win the frame. Had the player with two bocce balls attempted the hit and failed, he and his partner would then each have one chance to close in. The percentages, however, favor one player with two chances over two players with one chance each.

The Polaroid Approach & Positive Mental Imaging

In Chapter 3, we introduced what I'll call the Polaroid approach. Stand near the backboard and take a mental Polaroid, pause to let it come into focus, then block everything out and focus on the shot. Before executing, create a positive mental image of a well-placed shot. Get your teammates to avoid comments that create a negative image. "Don't be short of the pallino" gives an image of a shot that doesn't quite reach its intended destination. "Make it reach beyond the pallino" creates a different picture in the mind. The body aspires to the mental images it processes. We teach our baseball players not to say things like "Don't lose 'em!" when the pitcher gets behind in the count. We want to hear encouragement that produces positive images. "Throw strikes, big guy!" or "Toss it right down the middle of the plate like you can, Mark!" are what we want to hear and they create the images we want to visualize. There is a great deal of documentation supporting mental imagery as a valid tool for improving skills in basketball, football, swimming, karate, skiing, volleyball, tennis and golf. There is no reason it can't help your bocce.

Bocce — Simple Yet Elegant

Bocce is such a simple but elegant endeavor. On the surface it seems so elementary. Yet, as we have seen, it can involve sophisticated strategy and mental skills. Marco Cignarale is one of the growing breed of young and talented bocce players. While still a college student, he competed in the 1993 World Cup of Bocce. He played the conventional games of basketball and soccer in high school, and learned bocce in his dad's backyard court. At the age of fifteen, he took second place at the World Series of Bocce in Rome, New York, spending his $500.00 cash prize on a new stereo. Cignarale sums the game up nicely. "It's really a mind game," says Marco. "One little mistake and you're done!"

Some Simple Strategic Suggestions

Drawing 1

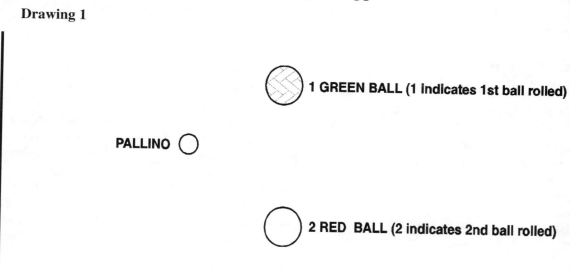

After green made the initial point, red tried to outlag or outpoint figuring that if he didn't close in he would spock on his next attempt. However, the roll was short, blocking his angle to spock the green point. So, a better strategy is to spock first and point next. Spock, miss and point is preferable to point, miss and spock.

Drawing 2

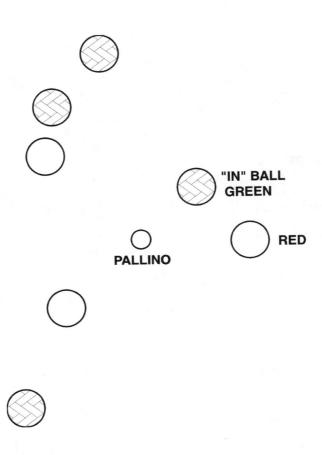

On the last ball, should red try to hit (spock) the green point and try for three or four points? If he misses and hits the red, then green gets a point. If he inadvertently hits the pallino to the backboard, green may score multiple points. Let the score, the situation, and the player's skill influence the decision.

Drawing 3

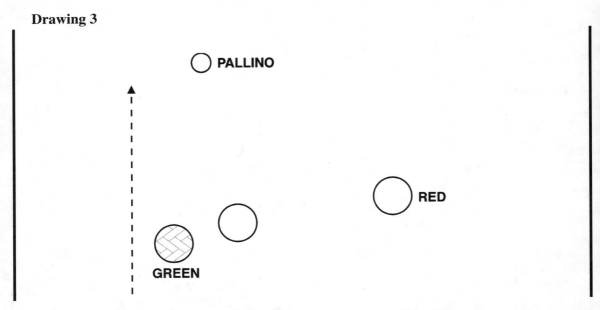

If green elects to roll for point, he should aim to the left of the pallino because this offers two positive options:

1.) The ball may close in for point to the left of the pallino.

2.) The ball may tap the green ball into scoring position.

Drawing 4

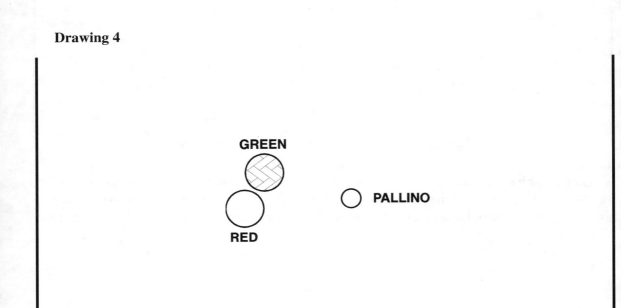

Red's next shot should be a strong roll since if it taps the red ball already played, it will carom into the green and knock it out of contention (leaving red with the possibility of two points).

Drawing 5

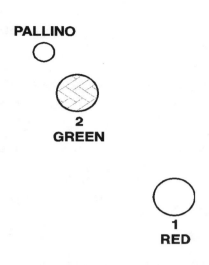

Red rolls first and makes a good point. Green rolls next and outpoints red. Red decides to spock (hit). Red should make the approach and delivery from the left side of the court to open up the widest target zone. The pallino may be knocked to the backboard from this angle or the green point may be hit away — both are positive options for red (if the pallino is hit to the backboard, chances are the red ball will follow it).

Drawing 6

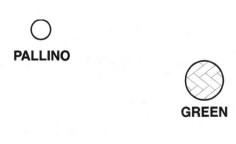

Red thinks he can outpoint green's shot but hits anyway because he knows that a miss will leave a red ball at the endboard as insurance against the opponents knocking the pallino there later in the frame.

Drawing 7

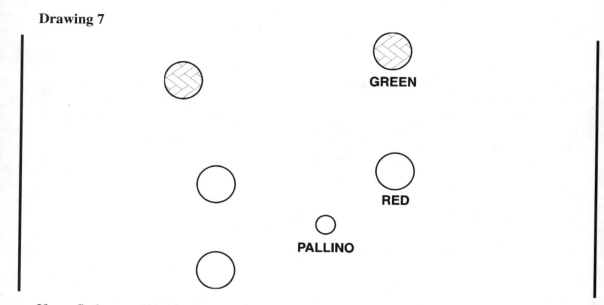

If you find yourself in the same position as the green team, you may want to make a strong roll at the pallino hoping to take it to the backboard for a possible two or three points.

Drawing 8

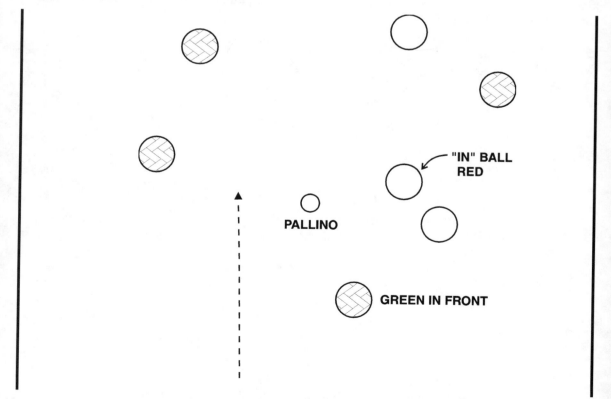

On red's last ball, stay left of the pallino — don't take a chance on hitting the green in front and "selling the point."

Drawing 9

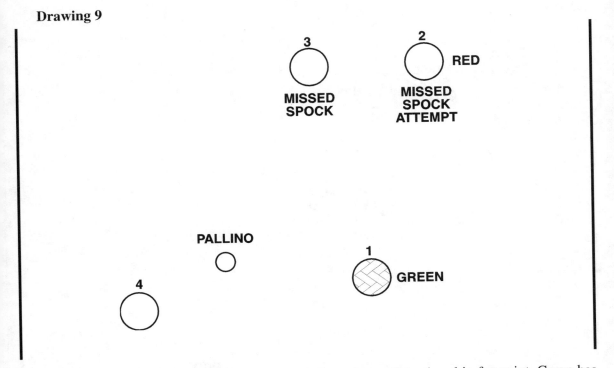

Green rolled initial point. Red missed two spock attempts, then closed in for point. Green has three balls left to red's one. Hit in this situation.

Drawing 10

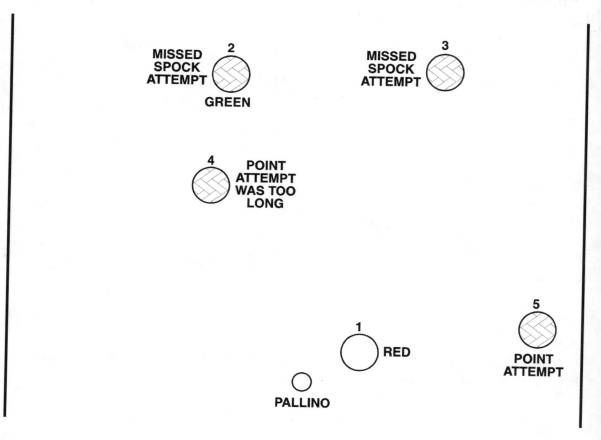

Green used all four balls and failed to take out or outpoint red's initial point. Red should stand to the left side of court and roll off the right sideboard. If not rolled too hard, the red ball should knock green #5 out and stay in for a point. The same type shot executed softly two more times should score four points for red. These are relatively easy shots and make for a better percentage shot than trying to outpoint #5.

Drawing 11

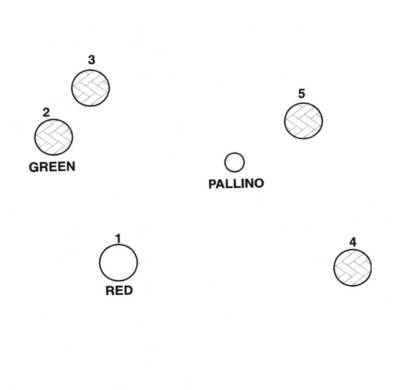

Green took four shots to outpoint red's initial point. With three balls left, red can either hit green's point (#5) or take the pallino to the backboard. Either way red should score multiple points.

Drawing 12

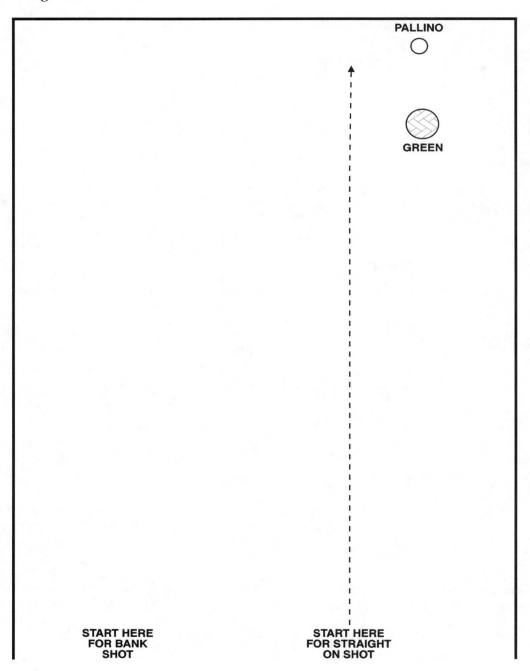

Green's point is short of the pallino and near the backboard. Red must decide whether to hit or point. If he elects to point there are two options:

1.) roll straight on — aim left of pallino so as not to tap green closer, or

2.) use bank shot.

Adjust your starting position accordingly.

Chapter 7
Building A Backyard Court

The following pages give step-by-step details for building a backyard court. To add insight to the process, photos and information are included chronicling the construction of my own family's court. Building my court served two purposes. It gave me the opportunity to advance to the next level of competition, and it gave me firsthand knowledge to better write this chapter on court construction. Comments concerning my backyard bocce court are separated from the text by a boxed outline.

You can have a great deal of enjoyment playing bocce without a professional-looking court on your premises, and thereby preserve your open space for other activities. One of the most attractive aspects of the sport has always been that it can be played by anyone almost anywhere. If you do opt for a court enclosed by sideboards and endboards, it is likely to be a permanent structure. The task of building a quality, permanent court is not to be taken lightly. To construct anything but the simplest of bocce courts, your yard is going to be in a state of disarray for weeks. Your lawn will likely be devastated by trucks delivering sand, gravel, stone dust or clay, and your relationship with significant others may be altered. You also need to consider the effect the alley's construction will have on the neighborhood. Will it be a welcome sight or an eyesore? Is there a chance that you'll someday put up spotlights for night play? How will this affect the neighborhood's tranquillity?

The Building Site

Once you've made the decision to build, spend some time deciding on its precise location. Side yard or backyard? Are there trees and shrubs that will have to be sacrificed? How does the land pitch from one end to the other? Where can you build that allows you to create the court that meets the dimensions you desire? Is one area more conducive to good drainage than another? Soil types and drainage patterns vary widely from one area to another (you can install perforated pipe to aid drainage). How will sunrise and sunset affect play? Some builders recommend that the court's length run north to south to prevent annoying glare at dawn and dusk.

The final site should be the rectangular piece of your property that comes closest to satisfying the above issues. You may have to make trade-offs. The most level area available to you may not be the most asthetically pleasing or the most convenient location for the alley. You may have to sacrifice or relocate favored trees or shrubs.

My family owns a home on a corner lot in a pleasant, family neighborhood. We debated the merits of building the court on our side yard (surrounded by a four-foot tall, split picket fence) vs. our backyard (enclosed by a six-foot chain link fence). We finally opted for the privacy afforded by the backyard, which also preserved our side yard's open space for other activities like softball, badminton, and bocce on the lawn. I had hoped for a 76 x 12 foot court, but settled for 76 x 10 because I wasn't willing to sacrifice a row of fruit trees that border the playing area. The compromise worked well since the line of trees gives a European ambiance to our alley.

The Dimensions

People always ask if a court is regulation or official size. The question is difficult to answer because different governing bodies mandate different court dimensions. Here on the East Coast there are many 12 x 60 foot courts. These were built according to International Bocce Association standards. The IBA, located in Utica, New York, has a well-devised set of rules, established in 1980, that still governs play in many tournaments on the East Coast. The group is well established and many people build courts to their official specifications. However, organizations in other areas prefer larger courts of 70 to 90 feet in length. True international court dimensions are 27.5 by 4 meters for volo rules play, and 26.5 by 3.8 to 4.5 for punto, raffa, volo rules competition. (We discuss these styles of play in Chapter 9, International Play). So, if you want a court that meets these specifications, you'll want one that is approximately 90 feet long by 13 feet wide.

You can build a court of any length and width that you desire, unless you plan to host a tournament. That tournament court will have to meet the specifications outlined in the governing body's rules. As we have stated, there are courts as short as 60 feet and as long as 90 feet or more. Widths run anywhere from eight feet to 14 feet or more. Another thing to factor into your decision is the cost. The bigger the court, the greater the expense for materials and construction.

How Long?

Many veteran players don't like the 60-foot courts, maintaining that they are too short and provide too small a playing area. IBA rules require the initial toss of pallino to come to rest on or beyond the half court marker (30 feet). Since a player may hit or spock from the 10-foot line, a target near midcourt may be as close as twenty feet away. Compounding the problem is that in many local tournaments, players get away with flagrantly violating the foul line. Their approach and delivery bring them practically on top of the ball they're trying to hit. Many bocce players prefer longer courts. The World Bocce Association (WBA), based in Illinois and the Wonderful World of Bocce Association (WWOBA) in Massachusetts have agreed on 76 feet as the standard length. This seems a good compromise between the 60- and 90-foot extremes. You have enough open court to make for challenging play, and the size is reasonable for a family's backyard.

How Wide?

Courts are as narrow as eight feet and as wide as 14 or more. Widening the court minimizes the luck factor and maximizes the need for skillful play. For example, picture a court eight feet wide with the pallino resting at one end right in the center of that width. Considering only the width, the worst possible shot a player could make will end up no more than about four feet to the left or right of the target. A wider court means more open space calling for more precise rolling. Ten to twelve feet is a reasonable width. WBA and WWOBA have agreed on 10- to 12-foot widths.

To make your decision on court dimensions, take all of the foregoing into consideration. Keep in mind the difference between a court for backyard, recreational use and one for league or international tournament play. If you want to represent your country in international play, construct the large court. Otherwise, build it to fit your situation, your yard and your pocketbook. Most of all, build the court that makes you happy. If you only have room for a small court, fine! Build it and enjoy it. Don't let the court's size diminish the joy of playing.

Another Trade-Off

Before we built our court, we played exclusively on our grassy side yard and became pretty good players. When we entered tournaments played on stone dust or clay courts, however, we regularly were trounced. Several months after completing our court, my son James and I competed in a tournament in Old Lyme, Connecticut on 76- by 12-foot courts. We played pretty well, winning several matches and competing well in those that we lost. The backyard court is clearly helping us get to the next level. But it's somewhat disturbing that we don't seem to play on the lawn any more. Lawn bocce is a wonderful game full of challenging natural obstacles. While in Connecticut for the above-mentioned tournament, we visited friends from the 1995 Special Olympics Bocce Committee at the home of Roger Lord. After a delightful cookout and reunion, we played lawn bocce. Roger has a world-class lawn for bocce. The course has rolling hills and some level areas and is just a delight to play on. You need to be able to roll, oh, so gently downhill and sometimes you have to heave the ball volo-like uphill. And you have to read the green like a golfer on the PGA tour. I had almost forgotten how much joy good friends and good lawn bocce could provide. Building a backyard court brings with it this trade-off. You are going to get better at competitive tournament-style bocce, but you are probably not going to play much on the lawn again.

Initial Grading

Once you have the site and court dimensions selected, stake out the area using wooden stakes and mason's line. The staked area should be slightly larger than the finished playing area to allow access for heavy equipment. You'll need to strip the entire area of sod and loam, probably digging up and removing 12 inches of material. Grading with a bulldozer, Bobcat, or front-end loader may be necessary. The final playing surface must be as level as possible to provide for the best possible playing conditions. Some suggest treating the stripped area with herbicide or putting down rolls of plastic landscape fabric to prevent new growth of grass or weeds coming up through the court surface. Let your environmental conscience be your guide in this matter.

Sideboards, Squaring the Court, Leveling the Boards

Once the playing area is stripped, reset the stakes to the precise play area measurements. Put up the sideboards now, using a transit, carpenter's level or line level. Leaving one endboard until last allows for easy access for a wheelbarrow or machinery to deliver and spread materials. The side and endboards may be of any material that will not move when struck by a ball. They must be at least as high as the balls (6-12 inches recommended). Both ends must be higher to protect spectators and players because most balls knocked out of the court exit near the ends. You can construct the

The different phases of court construction

court walls with landscaping timbers (6" x 6" or 8" x 8"), or wood planking. Pressure treated stock is highly recommended. Be sure to square the ends of the boards before installing them. To square the court, measure the diagonal distance between corner stakes. The lengths should be equal. Use a transit to mark the stakes at the appropriate height and secure the line tightly at these marks. For example, if you are using 12-inch high sideboards, mark one stake 12 inches from the subsurface and shoot your transit readings from that mark. Without a transit use the longest level you can obtain and, instead of marking the stakes, set one sideboard in place at a time using the mason line and leveling as you go along. Remember, save one of the endboards for last. Set the other side of the court along the mason's line, leveling it relative to the first side. Use a board long enough to reach across the width of the court for this job, reading the carpenter's level that is placed on top. Drive stakes two to three feet into the ground to shore up the boards and keep them straight. Use the mason's line to guide your work on the sideboards. Some builders recommend steel reinforcing rods $5/_8$ inch in diameter by 24 inches long if the side walls are three inches or thicker. The idea is to drill holes vertically down through the width of the boards every five or six feet, driving the rods into the ground until they are flush with the top of boards. With two inch or narrower boards you can use 1" x 24" rods. Drive these into the ground against the sideboards at five- to six-foot intervals and attach with u-bolt clamps. Use no reinforcing rods in the endboards since they experience the most wear and tear and are the most likely to need repair or replacement. Also, be aware that steel rods used externally will eventually rust.

Note: You may want to drill a small hole through the endboard to allow excessive water to drain after rainstorms. Drill the hole parallel to and just above the court's surface. This is important if you are running a tournament, and don't have time to wait for your court to dry out naturally.

The bocce court surface

The leveling process

After much deliberation, we decided to situate our court in the backyard between our chain link fence and row of apple and pear trees. We could attach the sideboards on one side to the existing fence posts. The court would have the chain-link fence on one side, and an attractive row of fruit trees on the other. One of the first problems we encountered was a 20-inch drop in elevation from one end of our proposed play area to the other. We shot a line with a transit and put up the sideboards as level as possible. We decided on pressure treated planking, using 2" x 12" x 16' boards. Setting five boards end to end on each side and would give us an 80-foot court that we could later cut back to 76 feet. We used the existing chain-link fence posts as stakes, attaching the boards to them with a post-to-fence bracket. The brackets were screwed into the sideboard with 1 $\frac{1}{2}$" galvanized decking screws and then fastened to the pipe with the hardware packaged with the bracket. On the opposite side of the court we drove galvanized steel pipes into the ground with a heavy sledge hammer and fastened the brackets around these and onto the sideboards. We used metal tie plates to align the joints of two abutting planks (top and bottom). The finished court is pictured on the previous page and we are extremely pleased. Hats off to my good friend and handyman, Joe Austin, who served as foreman and chief laborer on the job. Heck, the guy installed his own in-ground pool — I figured I could trust my bocce court to him.

With the sides up and the grass and loam removed, we went about bringing in the subsurface materials.

The Sub-Surface Materials

We recommend a five-inch layer of sand followed by three inches of crushed stone. This will ensure good drainage. Many builders skip the sand and use only gravel or crushed stone as a base. Other than #1 or #2 crushed stone, a gravel mix, or any mixture of pebbles, ground shell, sand or soil that provides adequate drainage may be used. Some builders recommend wetting and compacting the subsurface with a tamper or a gas-driven compactor. Others opt for doing the compacting only when the final surface is in place.

For this work we hired a contractor who used a front-end loader to spread and level the materials. We then screwed and/or toe nailed 10-foot two-by-fours across the width of the court at the bottom of the sideboards (see photo page 68). These two-by-fours, buried under the surface material, help reinforce the consistent 10-foot width of our court.

The Surface

Finally, spread three inches of surface material. You can use any surface material that is porous. Clay, packed earth, dirt, gravel, grass, indoor/outdoor carpet or other artificial surfaces are used. The most common surfaces, though, are clay and stone dust (screened stone dust preferred — $\frac{1}{8}$ inch screen recommended). Some builders suggest an additional top coat of 1 inch of brick dust or the very fine, sifted clay like what is used on tennis courts. Others recommend that the three-inch surface material be crushed limestone, baseball warning track clay, screened crushed sea shells, or a mixture of five parts clay to one part coarse or fine oyster shell. Another option is to use one of the previous materials as a one-inch top coat. If you opt for the one-inch topping, put it down in four applications of $\frac{1}{4}$ inch at a time. Wet and roll the material with a heavy roller between applications. The surface must be dry enough that it doesn't collect on the roller during this process.

We added three inches of stone dust, again using the heavy machinery to deliver and level the material. We wet and rolled the surface with a heavy roller, repeating the process daily. Playing games in between helps expose the high and low spots. We may let the surface settle for a season and then add an inch of either brick dust or fine sifted clay. Experienced players tell us that this clay is easily tracked into the house, so we may forgo it.

Leveling the Surface

Roll the surface with a heavy roller. Wet the surface down, let it dry, and roll again. After the initial rolling process, use an angle iron or a straight board about the width of the court and drag it lengthwise across the court. This scraping process, called screeting by concrete workers, removes high spots and fills in low points. Repeat this screeting process several times, wetting and rolling between each pass. You can also use a rigid rake 36 inches or more in width to scrape and grade the surface. These are sometimes called infield rakes because baseball grounds-keepers use them. They have teeth on one side, and a grading surface on the other (see photo).

Leveling the final surface takes some time and help from mother nature in the form of rainfall. A good soaking rainstorm speeds up the leveling process considerably by exposing low spots (puddles) that you can fill with additional material. A galvanized fence post the width of the court can also help with leveling. Set it down across the width of the court and place a four-foot carpenter's level on top of it. (See photo) Besides the feedback from the bubble in the level, low spots and irregularities show up clearly when light passes underneath the bar.

Initially, the surface will be soft enough so that a ball dropped from waist level or above will leave an indentation where it strikes the ground. Over time the surface should get harder and play faster. Volo shots that strike the surface will leave large, round indentations at first. As the court surface becomes harder, the size of the indentation will get smaller. These marks may start out the size of a softball on a new court. Eventually, they shrink to the size of a silver dollar, half dollar, and then a quarter. When they approximate the size of a dime, the court is fully settled.

Swingboards discourage rebound attempts off the endboard.

Swingboard Construction

Use two by tens slightly shorter than the court's width as swingboards. At each end of the court, suspend the boards just off the court surface using screw hooks that latch onto eye bolts inserted into the backboard (see photo). During play, these swingboards absorb the energy of raffa impacts, thus discouraging rebound attempts off the endboard. Usually, builders cover this board with a material (carpet, rubber, old fire hose) that adds to the "give" of the board and protects it from damage.

Extra Height at the Ends

To ensure that balls hit by raffa and volo attempts stay in the court, you will need additional height at the endboards and sideboards near both ends. You can accomplish this by adding additional tiers or levels of boards. Fasten these boards securely to the existing structure and brace them with wood stakes and/or metal brackets. Use galvanized screws, not nails. You will have to gauge how far out from the endboard to extend this added height (16 feet recommended). WWOBA recommends courts with an interesting staircase effect. The sideboards are one foot high. Starting at 12 feet from the endboard the height of the sides increases to three, four, then five feet high. (See photo page 75)

> We added a second tier of two-by-twelves to each end of our court. These extended 16 feet from each end. We fastened them with metal brackets and wood strips (see photo). Currently, we are waiting for a promised donation of old fire hose that we will fasten to the swingboard.

Extra height at the ends of the court help ensure balls stay in the court.

Tools and Materials Needed

landscaping timbers or planking for side and endboards (pressure treated)
steel reinforcing rods or other means for staking boards
sand
crushed stone
surface material (clay, stone dust, or other screened topping)
heavy machinery (backhoe, Bobcat, etc.)
pick
shovel
rake
hammer
sledge hammer
ax (for tree or root removal)
transit
four foot or longer carpenter's level
line level
mason's line
framing square
100-foot steel tape measure
heavy lawn roller
L-shaped framing brackets and metal tie plates
screws (not nails) 1 $^1/_2$- and 3-inch galvanized decking screws
9- or 12-volt battery operated screw gun AC/DC
circular saw

Court Markings

Depending on whose rules you intend to play by, your court markings will be different. Some groups like WWOBA play with one foul line that is both for pointing and hitting. The line is 20 feet from each end. For IBA rules played on 60-foot courts, you'll need a foul line for pointing four feet from each backboard, and a foul line for hitting 10 feet from each backboard. For WBA play on 76-foot courts, you'll want pointing lines six feet from the ends and hitting lines at the 10-foot marks. Hopefully, as the game continues to grow, a standard will emerge that will be embraced by all the various groups. At any rate, the lines are generally painted on both sideboards. (See photo page 14) You may also want to (especially for tournament play) put down a chalk line on the surface much like a baseball foul line.

For international play, the pointing and raffa line is four meters from the endboard, while the volo line is seven meters from the end. See Chapter 9 for international rules and contact the United States Bocce Federation (see Chapter 5) for additional information on international courts and tournament play.

Most rules call for the initial toss of the pallino to come to rest at or beyond midcourt. You will need to paint this line on both sideboards as well. Again, for league or tournament play you may want a chalk line running across the surface.

Finally, many rules call for the pallino to come to rest a minimum distance from the backboard. IBA rules mandate four feet from the backboard, WWOBA rules call for three feet. The Open Rules outlined in Chapter 8 are gaining momentum and they contain no such restriction except that the initial toss of pallino not touch the backboard.

I prefer one line for hitting and pointing and this works well on the larger 76-foot court. WWOBA's 20-foot line is too far for my tastes. I opted for a 10-foot foul line that coincides with WBA and IBA, but also painted a six-foot line for pointing WBA style and a four-foot line for IBA. I don't like all these different lines, but I want to be able to use my court to prepare for tournament play governed by both groups.

Some Interesting Options

You may want to consider spectator benches for your court. They should be placed carefully, considering both the fans' view of the game and their safety. Fewer balls fly out of the court near the center than at the ends, so caution dictates that they be placed accordingly. Some bocce players install angle boards (45 degrees from each side to the endboard) that can be used for ricochet and carom shots. Others favor a bumper board over a swingboard. This bumper board doesn't swing, but acts as a shock absorber, collecting the energy of a fast moving ball. Still others use a ditch instead of an endboard. If your ball ends up in the ditch, it is dead. Finally, consider leaving a cutout or removable section somewhere along your sideboards to allow for both handicap access as well as easy entry and exit for your heavy roller.

Synthetic courts may bring the game to yet another level. Not only is there almost no maintenance involved, but the game becomes very clean. I mean, your hands don't even get dirty. If synthetic surfaces (poured rubber, indoor/outdoor carpet, artificial turf) become the rage and the game flourishes the way aficionados think it will, the sport will likely welcome the designer clothes market.

Freestanding (portable) courts represent still another option. These can be assembled in twenty minutes or so, played on, and then broken down for storage. Portable courts can be set up outdoors on a level patch of grass or earth, or indoors on composition floors like in a school gymnasium. They are used to conduct tournaments in hotels and convention halls. Courts are set up on the hotel carpet for example, with the carpet becoming the playing surface. After the tournament, the court is dismantled and the hotel has its hall or meeting room back.

A group that I belong to commissioned a tradesman to build a portable court of wood construction. It can be assembled by several people in about twenty minutes using only ratchet sets. We set it up in our high school fieldhouse that has a poured rubber floor and use it for intramurals and for adult evening play in the winter. When finished playing, we disassemble it so that it doesn't interfere with physical education classes or other sports teams' practices. We figure that bocce poses no threat to the composition floor since they heave the 16-pound shot there during track meets. We're hoping to sell the physical education teachers on bocce as a class unit.

Court Maintenance

A well-constructed court should pose only a minimal maintenance problem. The court needs to be groomed after use by brooming, rugging (dragging a rug attached to a rope), or otherwise dragging the surface. The broom, rug, or other device used should be at least 24 inches wide. Thirty-six to 48 inches or more would be preferable to allow for the fewest number of passes when grooming. Fewer passes mean less work and fewer seams where material might collect.

Occasionally you will have to wet and roll the surface. This will be anywhere from once a month to once a week depending on how much use your court gets. Be sure to examine the surface right after rainstorms and fill in any low spots. In the spring you may have to do an annual screeting and some realignment of the sideboards. Occasionally, an endboard that has taken its share of raffas needs to be repaired or replaced.

Bocce courts require a small amount of maintenance, including grooming.

Court Construction Synopsis

1. Pick the site.
2. Decide on dimensions.
3. Stake out an area larger than the actual playing area using wooden stakes and mason's line.
4. Strip the area of sod and dirt (12 inches).
5. Reset stakes to actual court dimensions.
6. Put up sideboards using transit, carpenter's level, or line level, leaving one end board for last.
7. Bring in and spread subsurface materials.
8. Bring in and spread surface materials.
9. Compact and level surface using the screeting process, raking, wetting, and heavy roller.
10. Add final end board and additional tiers for desired height.
11. Install swingboard.
12. Paint court markings.
13. Revel in the outdoors and the joy of bocce.

Two examples of bocce courts

Different types of bocce scoreboards. The upper left scoreboard is interesting because one hand of the clock is red and the other is green so only one clock is needed to keep both teams' scores.

Chapter 8
Tournament Play & Rules

Advancing to the tournament level carries with it a trade-off. You gain the more serious competition that you may desire, but you lose the easy, relaxed atmosphere of play in your backyard, neighborhood park, or the beach. Where there was no pressure, no spectators lining the court, no prize money on the line, there is now a whole different ball game. With a little research, you can probably find some friendly tournament action, but there is also a good deal of high-level (some might even call it cutthroat) competition. The spectrum runs from those like the low-key "Play for the Prosciutto" tourney in Leominster, Massachusetts ($25.00 per team entry fee — 1st place actually wins a prosciutto) to those like the World Bocce League's Superball Classic in Rosemont, Illinois ($200+ per person entry fee includes hotel accommodations — winners collect $30,000 prize). It's probably a good idea to start at the "prosciutto level" and advance as your skills improve. Many local tournaments feature a relaxed atmosphere with good-natured competition. The players referee their own games, only summoning a tournament official in case of a close measurement or other dispute.

Before you enter a tournament, you should find out certain facts. Call the tournament director, or send for the tourney flier. You'll need to know the tournament format. Is it single elimination (one loss and you're out) or double (two losses)? Is the event for singles, doubles, or four-person teams? If it is for four-player teams, do the players throw two balls each and stay at one end of the court, or do they play one ball each and play both ends of the alley? Can you bring an additional player to serve as a substitute? What is the winning score in each game...12, 15, 16? On what type surface will the event be played — stone dust, clay, synthetics, carpet (some tournaments are run in hotels with temporary courts set up on the wall-to-wall carpeting)? Will the games be indoors or out? What are the dates and rain dates, if any? Is there prize money (tournament purses are mushrooming as bocce gains in popularity)? If so, how many teams finish "in the money?" How many games do you have to win to make it to the "money round?"

Many local tournaments return virtually all of the money collected from entry fees as prize money. They rely on the bar and concession sales to turn a profit. For example, one Massachusetts club hosted a 32-team event, collecting $100 per team for a total of $3200 in entry fees. The winners collected cash prizes on the following scale:

1st place =$1250

2nd place =$600

3rd place =$400

4th place =$250

5th place=$150

6th place=$150

7th place=$100

8th place= $100

Total prize money = $3000 with eight of 32 teams (25%) finishing "in the money."

As you can see, you are going to have to adjust to different court surfaces and other situations to make it on the tourney circuit. Once you get the details and decide to enter a tournament, you'll have to line up teammates and send in your application with entry fee. If you have a substitute (a fifth player in a four-member team) the captain must decide who plays in which game(s). Most tournament team captains recommend playing the best players in the early games, using the substitute later. The hope is that the stronger team will keep them out of the losers' bracket as long as possible. When you drop out of the winners' bracket early in a double elimination tourney, it makes it very tough to finish in the money.

Probably the most important question you'll need answered is, "What rules will govern the tournament's play?" Quite generally, the game is played the same way in close geographical areas. It is when you travel to another area that problems are likely to arise. A social club hosting a tournament will use its version of the game as the "official" tournament rules, and there may be any number of house rules observed. The winning score, for example, may be 11, 12, 15, 16 or more. Recently, at a tournament in Connecticut, I chatted with an animated senior citizen visiting from Florida. She was a regular on the bocce courts in her retirement home in the Sunshine State, but refused to play in this event. "I hate this tournament!" she said. "I don't like the rules they use," she explained. "The games should go to 11, not 12, and tournament games should go to 21."

"Tournament games to 21?" I asked. "That must take forever."

"Oh," she replied without missing a beat. "We have lots of time at the senior center."

In some areas, most notably the West Coast, international rules are observed (see Chapter 9, International Play). Increasingly, we are seeing tournaments governed by "open rules." These are modified from international rules, eliminating some of the restrictions that complicate and slow the game down. Strict international play calls for marking the positions of balls when a knockaway shot is to be taken. The player must call his shot and, if he fails to hit his target, any scattered balls may be returned to their original positions. Open rules are rapidly gaining popularity in this country. And though one group's idea of open rules might be slightly different from another's, they are very similar. Following are reprinted the World Bocce Association's Open Rules, first a general overview, then the full text. The WBA has edited and revised the full text of the rules thoroughly and completely, making every effort to cover every circumstance that might take place in a game.

Open Rules - General Overview

What follows is a general overview of open rules as used in league and tournament play. As you might expect, the regulations get a little more stringent than what we outlined in Chapter 1, but are a far cry from the international rules that require referees to mark the positions of balls every time a player attempts to knock a ball away.

Reprinted with permission of the World Bocce Association, Philip Ferrari, President

Revised 9/95

{Comments in brackets are the author's}

1. Composition balls will be used. Sizes suggested are 107 to 114 millimeters in diameter, with weights between 920 and 1100 grams.
2. The toss of the coin will decide the starting team and the winner will also choose the color of the balls. {The winners of the coin toss get control of the pallino and their choice of the color of balls — some versions of open rules give the winner of the toss the choice of first toss of pallino or the color of balls.}
3. The starting team must toss the "pallino" to a valid position past the center or "in play" line, but not coming to rest on the backboard. It must settle at least 12 inches from the sideboard. If, after three attempts, the starting team fails to validly place it, the opposing team tosses the pallino. If the opposing team fails in the first attempt, the referee will place the pallino in a valid position. The first bocce ball is rolled by the player who originally tossed the pallino.
4. The pallino remains in play unless it is knocked out of the court or in front of the center or "in play" line, then the frame is ended and play resumes from the opposite end. The same team tosses the pallino. {The team that tossed the pallino for the canceled frame tosses it again, restarting from the opposite end.}
5. A ball touching the backboard is dead unless it first strikes another ball, in which case all balls are valid. {Any shot, whether punto, raffa, or volo that goes to the backboard without first striking another ball is dead and removed from the court — different groups playing open rules seem to be moving in this direction.}
6. If the first thrown ball of the starting team touches the backboard without first hitting the pallino, the ball is out of play and that team must roll again until the initial point is established.
7. A thrown ball that doesn't touch another ball and returns from the backboard into the field of play and strikes another ball and/or the pallino is out of play. The pallino and/or the other balls are returned to their approximate original positions. If a ball strikes the backboard causing a ball or balls resting on the backboard to move, the ball(s) are returned to their approximate original positions. {This is a common occurrence when previously played balls are in contact with the swingboard.}
8. The players shall not step over the foul line before releasing the pallino or their ball.
9. Players may use the sideboard at any time.
10. The tournament host will decide on the number of points required to win a match.
11. All players must remain outside the court while the opposing team is rolling.

12. In a tournament game when substitutes are allowed, a team may make one substitution from their roster per game. This substitution may take place at any time in a game. Once a player has been removed from a game, the player cannot reenter that same game.

13. Volo shooting is lofting the ball in the air beyond the center or "in play" line of the court. Volo shooting is only allowed on courts where the in play line for first toss of pallino is at least 38 feet from the backboard. {WBA reasons that, with a longer play area, volo attempts are not easy targets as they are on the shorter courts. Note that to qualify as a volo, the attempt must first land past the center line}

14. In the case of a tie between two balls, the prevailing (or first ball) has to be beaten, not tied. If the frame ends in a tie, no points are awarded and play resumes from the opposite end of the court with the same team tossing the pallino.

15. If a player rolls the wrong colored ball, simply replace it with the correct color when the ball comes to rest.

16. If a player rolls out of turn, the opposing team may leave everything, including the thrown ball, exactly as is or may return any moved balls to their approximate positions and remove the thrown ball. {This option of accepting the play, or returning displaced balls to their original positions and "killing" the illegally thrown ball, is bocce's *rule of advantage*. The option goes to the opponents of the team that commits the infraction.}

17. If an individual delivers more than his allotted number of balls, the opposing team may accept the result of the illegal roll, or remove the illegal ball and return any scattered balls to their original positions. {Bocce's *rule of advantage* applies.}

18. Team captains may request measurement of any ball at any time.

19. Any and all disputes will be resolved by the tournament committee.

20. When hitting, mark the positions of all balls that are three feet or less from the backboard. {If the ball hits a ball on its way to the backboard, it is live and the play stands. If it contacts no ball and then hits the backboard, it is dead and removed from the court. This rule #20 is necessary because of a third possible scenario. The ball may hit no ball, strike the backboard, and then carom into a ball or balls near the endboards. These displaced balls have to be returned to their original locations and therefore those positions must be marked previous to the shot.}

World Bocce Association Open Rules — Complete Text

(Reprinted with permission of the World Bocce Association) Revised 9/95
The World Bocce Association has adapted and revised these rules from several existing sets of regulations including those of the International Bocce Association, the United States Bocce Federation and the Special Olympics.

RULE 1: DEFINITIONS

ARTICLE 1 - Ball: Live and Dead

Section 1 - A Live Ball is any ball that has been legally delivered and is in play.

Section 2 - A Dead Ball is any ball that has been disqualified. A ball may be disqualified if it:

- is the result of a penalty
- has gone out of the court
- has come into contact with a person or object that is out of the court
- hits the top of the court boards
- hits the covering or support of the courts
- hits the backboard without first striking a ball on the court

ARTICLE 2 -Bocce Ball and Pallino

Section 1 - The Pallino is the small ball that serves as the object or target toward which the bocce balls are rolled. It is sometimes known as the cue ball, jack, pill, or beebee.

Section 2 - The Bocce Ball is the larger of the playing balls. There are four matched balls to a set. Bocce balls are used to score points or to displace an opponent's ball or the pallino.

ARTICLE 3 - Other Terms

Section 1 - Pointing refers to the act of delivering a ball to gain a position closest to the pallino in order to score a point.

Section 2 - The Pointing Line is one of two foul lines on each end of the court. A player who intends to deliver the ball to score a point must release it somewhere between the backboards and the pointing line (located six feet from the backboard).

Section 3 - Hitting, also known as spocking, shooting, popping, and bombing, refers to a delivery that is thrown with sufficient velocity that the ball would hit the backboard if it missed its target. Hitting is usually used to move another ball out of position.

Section 4 - The Shooting Line is one of the two foul lines on each end of the court. A player who is hitting or spocking may deliver the bocce ball anywhere between the backboard and the shooting line without committing a foul.

Section 5 - A Bank or Rebound Shot refers to playing a ball off either the sideboards or the backboards.

Section 6 - The Initial Point refers to the first ball that is rolled toward the pallino at the start of a frame. Since this is the first ball, it is the closest to the pallino, and represents the initial point. The player that tosses the pallino at the start of a frame must always establish the initial point.

Section 7 - The Initial Roll is the first delivery after the pallino is tossed to start a new frame. The player tossing the pallino is always responsible for making the initial roll. If the first thrown ball of the starting team touches the backboard without first hitting the pallino, the ball is out of play and that team must roll again until the initial point is established.

Section 8 - The In Team is the team whose ball is closest to the pallino. When a team is designated the "In Team," its players step aside and allow the opponents to play their balls.

Section 9 - The Out Team is the team that is not closest to pallino. The out team must deliver the next ball.

Section 10 - A frame is the period in a game when both teams deliver their bocce balls from one side of the court to the other and points are awarded. There is no set number of frames in a game, as a point total determines the winner.

Section 11- Pallino Advantage refers to possessing the right to start a frame by tossing the pallino and the first ball. Pallino advantage is determined at the start of a game by a coin toss. Subsequently, the team that wins each frame by scoring a point (or points) also wins pallino advantage for the next frame.

ARTICLE 4 - Fouls

Section 1 - A Foul is an infraction of the rules which carries a penalty.

Section 2 - A Foul Line Foul or Foot Foul is a situation during a delivery in which a player oversteps the foul line before releasing the ball.

Section 3 - A Moving Ball or Pallino Foul is a situation in which a player delivers his/her ball before the previous player's ball or the pallino has come to rest.

Section 4 - An Illegal Movement Foul is a situation in which a player moves a ball or the pallino by means other than the normal play. Touching or kicking a ball before the frame is completed are examples of illegal movement.

RULE 2: THE COURT AND EQUIPMENT

ARTICLE 1 - The Court and Markings

Section 1 - The Court shall be a rectangular surface measuring 76 feet in length and 10 to 12 feet in width. Detailed construction plans can be obtained from the World Bocce Association, LTD.

Section 2 - The Court Surface may be composed of stone-dust, dirt, clay, grass or artificial surface providing there are no obstructions on the court that may interfere with the straight-line delivery of a ball from any direction. Variations in grade or consistency of terrain are not considered obstructions.

Section 3 - The Walls of the Court may be composed of wood or any rigid material which withstands the ball's impact and which allows the balls to rebound off the surface. The height must be at least eight inches from the finish surface at all points. Side walls with removable sections allowing handicap access are highly recommended.

Section 4 - Court Markings must be clearly visible. They should be painted at the proper positions on the side boards. Each painted line should be at least two inches wide and should run from the court surface to the top of the sideboard.

Section 5 - Foul Lines shall be marked: (see diagram, next page, for placement)

a) For Pointing - six feet from the backboards on each side of the court so that an imaginary line is formed across the court perpendicular to the sideboards and parallel to the endboards.

b) For Hitting - ten feet from the backboards on each side of the court so that an imaginary line is formed across the court perpendicular to the sideboards and parallel to the endboards.

Section 6 - In-bounds lines shall be marked for the first toss of the pallino. The pallino must come to rest at least 12 inches from the sideboards and cannot touch the backline or backboards.

Section 7 - A Halfcourt Line shall be marked (see diagram, next page, for placement) at midcourt or 38 feet from the endboards so that an imaginary line is formed across the center of the court and perpendicular to the sideboards. The initial toss of pallino must be beyond this line. If, during play, the pallino is subsequently hit and it comes to rest in front of this line, the frame is dead and play starts over from the opposite end.

ARTICLE 2 - Court Grooming

Section 1 - Prior to Play, all courts must be groomed to the satisfaction of the Tournament Directors. If the court is composed of materials such as stone-dust, dirt or clay, a broom or rug at least four feet in width should be used to drag the surface.

Section 2 - Court Grooming After Play Has Begun is not permitted. However, obstacles or foreign objects such as stones, cups or other debris which would affect play may be removed.

Section 3 - Unusual Court Conditions which tournament directors feel negatively affect play can result in the game being halted and rescheduled on another court.

ARTICLE 3 - The Equipment

Section 1 - The Bocce Ball may be of composition, wood, or metal. The size of the balls may vary from 107 to 114 millimeters in diameter and between 920 and 1100 grams in weight. The balls being used by a team, however, must be exactly the same size and of the same material. Bocce balls may be any color provided a team's set of balls matches and are of a different color than that of their opponents.

Section 2 - The Pallino or target ball may not be larger than 63mm (2 1/2') or smaller than 53mm (2 1/8"). The pallino may be any color as long as it is in sharp contrast to the colors of the bocce balls in a game.

Section 3 - The Measuring Device is a steel tape that has the capacity to reach at least 12 feet. Tournament Directors may approve other devices for measuring distances which are too small to be measured accurately by the steel tape.

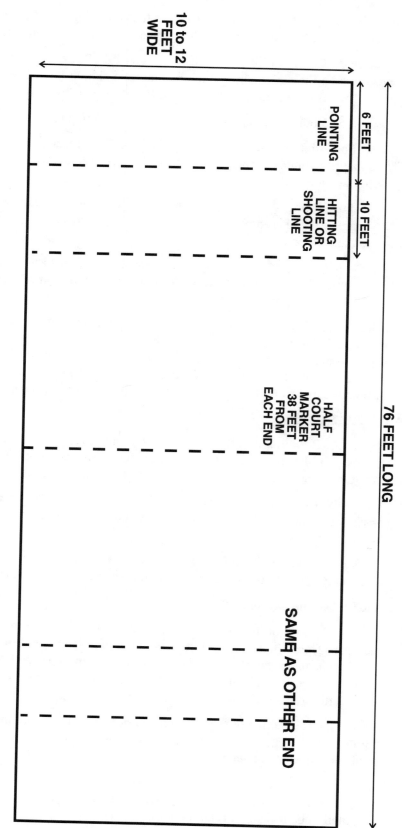

10 to 12 FEET WIDE

76 FEET LONG

6 FEET

10 FEET

POINTING LINE

HITTING LINE OR SHOOTING LINE

HALF COURT MARKER 38 FEET FROM EACH END

SAME AS OTHER END

Not drawn to scale

Section 4 - The Scoreboard may be freestanding or be posted at eye level at the end of the court in a manner that does not disturb play. Two sets of numbers at least 8 inches high shall be displayed on each board and shall be numbered consecutively from 0 to 16. The boards may be electronic or manual. There should be some means of differentiating between teams either by posting home vs. away status, team names, or assigning different colored numbers to each team.

RULE 3: PLAYERS AND SUBSTITUTIONS

ARTICLE 1 - Players

Section 1 - A Team (depending on the type of tournament) may consist of one, two, or four players plus one substitute and a coach.

Section 2 - At least 10 minutes before the scheduled game's starting time, each team shall supply the official with the names of the starting players and, if the team has one, the name of the substitute.

Section 3 - The Captain of each team must be designated and made known to the officials before play begins. The captain may not be changed during the game, but may be changed during the course of a tournament or league. Tournament or league officials must be notified of any such change of captains.

ARTICLE 2 - Substitution

Section 1 - Only one substitute is allowed per team per game.

Section 2 - Substitution may take place at any time. Once a player has been removed from a game for a substitution, the player cannot reenter that same game.

Section 3 - A Player who has registered to substitute for a particular team during a tournament may not substitute for another team during that tournament.

Section 4 - If an illegal substitute is used, the offending team shall forfeit the game.

ARTICLE 3 - Uniforms

Section 1 - Matching Shirts shall be worn by all players. Although a color is not specified, white is preferred. Teams may wear either short sleeve or long sleeve shirts as long as all members of the team are identically dressed.

Section 2 - A World Bocce Association logo must be placed over the area of the left shirt pocket. Lettering may appear, with the written permission from World Bocce Association, on the back of the shirts.

Section 3 - Matching team pants shall be worn by all players. Although a color is not specified, white is preferred. In warm weather, teams may wear shorts as long as every member of the team is identically dressed.

Section 4 - Sneakers shall be worn by all players. The soles of the sneakers should allow maximum traction for the player without causing undue damage to the court. Leather soled shoes or shoes with cleats are not allowed.

RULE 4: PLAY OF THE GAME

Section 1 - Equipment - Bocce is played with eight large balls and one smaller target or object ball called the pallino. The bocce balls are divided into two units of four balls each. Each unit is a different color. A side or team is designated a particular color at the start of the game and is given the appropriate color balls to use. The large balls are all inscribed with distinctive lines to identify the balls of the players on the same team.

Section 2 - Pallino and Color - A coin toss by the referee will determine which side will toss the pallino to begin the game and which team rolls which color ball. The team winning the toss gets both options. In the absence of a referee, the team coaches and captains shall execute the coin toss.

Section 3 - Start of the Game - To start the game, a member of the team who has won the coin toss rolls the pallino into play. After the pallino comes to rest in a legal position (beyond midcourt, at least 12 inches from the sideboard, and not touching the backboard), the player delivering the pallino must then deliver the first ball to establish the initial point.

Section 4 - Sequence of Play - The team with the pallino advantage (the team that won the previous frame) starts each frame by legally delivering the pallino and the first ball. As in the start of the game, the player delivering the pallino must be the one to deliver the first ball. That team will become the "In Team" because their ball is closest to the pallino.

After the pallino and first ball are delivered, the opposing team or "Out Team" delivers a ball in an attempt to position their ball closest to the pallino. If they are successful, they step aside and allow the other team to deliver. If they are unsuccessful, they remain the "Out Team" and continue to deliver until they become the "In Team" or they have exhausted their four balls.

The "nearest ball" rule governs the sequence of played balls. The side whose ball is closest to the pallino is called the "in" ball and the opposing side the "out" ball. Whenever a team gets "in" it steps aside and allows the "out" team to deliver.

Section 5 - Pallino Delivery - Legal delivery of the pallino can be accomplished by rolling, tossing, bouncing, or banking the pallino down the court so that it comes to rest in-bounds. In-bounds refers to any area beyond the midcourt line and at least 12 inches from the sideboards, but not touching the endboard. The pallino must be released by an underhand delivery and before the player crosses the foul line to be legal.

Section 6 - Three Attempt Rule - The team possessing the pallino will have three attempts at placing the pallino in-bounds at the start of the frame. If they are unsuccessful after three attempts, the opposing team will have one opportunity to legally place the pallino. If both teams are unsuccessful, the referee will place the pallino in the center of the opposite end "Hitting Line" or 66-foot mark.

No matter who legally sets the pallino, the team that had earned the pallino advantage in the previous frame delivers the first ball.

Section 7 - Initial Point - It is always incumbent upon the team with the pallino advantage to establish the initial point. EXAMPLE: Team A tosses the pallino and delivers the first ball to establish the initial point. Team B elects to hit Team A's ball and Team B's ball flies out of the court leaving only the pallino in the court. Team A must then deliver the next ball to reestablish the initial point.

Section 8 - Ball Delivery - A team has the option of rolling, tossing, bouncing, banking etc. their ball down the court provided it does not go out-of-bounds or the player does not violate the foul markers. A player also has the option of "Raffa" or "Volo," or hitting out any ball in play in trying to obtain a point, or decreasing the opposing team's points. Volo shooting is only allowed on courts where the in play line for first toss of pallino is at least 38 feet from the backboard. All ball delivery must be underhand style.

When hitting, mark the positions of all balls that are three feet or less from the backboard. If the raffa or volo attempt hits a ball on its way to the backboard, it is live and the play stands. If it hits the backboard without first touching another ball, it is dead and removed from the court. If after striking the backboard without first touching another ball, it then caroms into a ball or balls near the endboards, these displaced balls must be returned to their original locations. If a ball strikes the backboard and causes a ball or balls resting on the backboard to move, the ball(s) are returned to their approximate original positions.

To legally deliver the ball, the player may stay behind the pointing line when delivering a pointing shot and behind the hitting line when delivering a hitting shot. The players may legally step over the foul lines during follow-through if they have already released the ball.

Section 9 - Scoring - At the end of each frame (when both teams have delivered all four of their balls) points will be determined as follows: One point shall be awarded to each of the balls of one team that are closer to the pallino than the closest ball of the opposing team. This will be determined by the referee either by direct viewing or mechanical measuring.

The referee will be responsible for checking the accuracy of the scorecard and the scoreboard after every frame. It is incumbent upon the coach to verify the accuracy of the score at all times.

Section 10 - Measuring - When the pallino advantage or scoring cannot be accomplished easily by direct viewing, a mechanical means of measuring must be used. Team captains may request measurement of any ball at any time. When using a steel tape measure the zero end of the tape should be placed at the widest surface of the ball being measured. The tape then should be stretched so that it extends across the top of the pallino. The tape should be read at the top-center of the pallino. For closer measurements, tournament officials may approve an inside measure device (Reference Rule 2, Article 3, Section 3).

Section 11 - Ties During Frame - In the event the two opposing balls are equidistant from the pallino (tied), the team that rolled last will continue to roll until the tie is broken. EXAMPLE: If Team A rolls a ball for the pallino, then Team B rolls its ball for the pallino and the referee determines that both are exactly 13" away from the pallino, Team B must continue to roll until it has a ball closer to the pallino or it has exhausted its balls. If Team B does gain the pallino advantage and Team A hits their ball away, reestablishing a tie, then Team A must continue to roll until the tie is broken.

Section 12 - Ties at the End of the Frame - In the event that the two closest balls to the pallino belong to opposing teams and they are tied, no points shall be awarded and the pallino shall be returned to the team that delivered it originally. The new frame shall be played from the opposite side of the court on which the previous frame was played.

Section 13 - Winning Score - The number of points needed to win a game varies with the type of game being played. Final games go to 15 points and all preliminary rounds go to 12 points. A game is won when a side or team reaches:

- 15 points in a four-player team where one ball is delivered per player
- 12 points in a four-player team where two players stationed at each end of the court deliver two balls each
- 12 points in a two-player game where each player delivers four balls
- 12 points in a one-player game where one player delivers four balls

Section 14 - Scorecard - It is the responsibility of the coaches to sign the scorecard after a game and the signatures will indicate the indisputability of the final score. If a protest will be filed, the coaches disagreeing with the validity of the score should not sign the scorecard.

Section 15 - Scorekeeping - The scorekeeper should record the score on the scoreboard at the end of every frame.

Section 16 - Rotation of Players - The players of any given team may elect to play their ball in any rotation provided the player who tosses the pallino delivers the first ball. The rotation may vary from frame to frame; however, no player may deliver more than his/her allotted number of balls per game. (Refer to Rule 4, Section 13)

Section 17 - Position of Players - Only the player delivering a ball is allowed on the court. Other players must stay off the court until it is their turn to play. When all the balls have been delivered in a frame, the players may walk to the opposite side of the court. Players may not change positions or talk while another player is delivering the ball.

Section 18 - Position of Coaches - A team may have a coach stationed on both ends of the court. The coach at the near end where the players are playing out a frame may not step onto the court. He/she may coach from outside the court. The coach at the far end may provide coaching instruction, but may not enter the court nor may he/she move closer to the near side than the hitting lane.

Section 19 - Forfeiture - Teams with less than the prescribed number of players will forfeit the game. Also, when tournament officials inform a team that their court is ready for play, said team must be ready to start their game within 15 minutes or they shall forfeit the match.

RULE 5: TIME-OUTS, DELAYS-OF-GAME and CHECKING POSITION OF POINTS

ARTICLE 1 - Circumstances

Section 1 - Time-out - The official may grant a time-out whenever the circumstances explained by the team requesting the time-out appear to be valid. The time-out period will be limited to ten minutes. A team may only request a time-out if they are the "out" team, unless it is an emergency.

Section 2 - Intentional Delay-of-Game - If, in the opinion of the official, the game is intentionally delayed without sufficient or valid reason, the official will give a warning. If the game is not resumed within one minute of notification by the referee, the delaying team will forfeit the game.

Section 3 - Delays Caused by Weather, Acts of God, Civil Disorder, or Other Unforeseen Reasons - In such delays, the ruling of at least four directors of the tournament will rule and govern the final decision.

Section 4 - Checking Position of Points - Players may only proceed to the half-court mark to check the position of the balls before delivering their own ball(s).

Exceptions: In one-player teams, players may proceed down court at any time to observe conditions.

In two-player teams, one player may proceed down court to observe conditions.

When only one team has exhausted all of its balls, the referee shall not be permitted to declare, by measuring or viewing, which team is "in."

RULE 6: PENALTIES

ARTICLE 1 - Enforcement of Penalties

Section 1 - Determination - Immediately upon determination by the official that a foul has been committed, he/she will notify the coaches and captains of both teams and inform them of the penalty imposed. The ruling of the official is final, except as otherwise provided hereafter.

Section 2 - Conditions Not Covered - For conditions not specifically covered in these rules, at least four Tournament Directors will convene to render a decision. This decision shall be final.

Section 3 - Protests - Any protest of a decision of the officials or Tournament Director must be made by a team before that team plays its next ball or the decision will be considered accepted.

Section 4 - Protest to Forfeiture - If a team must forfeit a game as a result of not being present or on time for a scheduled game or as a result of violations hereunder prescribed, no official protest shall be acknowledged. Protests will be acknowledged and judged on the basis of merit in circumstances not specifically provided for hereunder.

ARTICLE 2 - Specific Fouls

Section 1 - Foul-line Fouls - In both pointing and hitting, the foremost part of the specific foul-line will not be surpassed by any part of the foot before the ball leaves the player's hand. All fouls must be called by the referee as a result of witnessing the foul.

One official warning may be granted a player after which penalties will be prescribed. The penalty for committing a second foul-line foul in a game will be removal of the ball from play. In addition, all balls displaced by this illegal toss must be returned to their approximate positions before the foul.

Section 2 - Illegal Movement of a Ball Belonging to Your Own Team - If a player moves one or more of his/her team's balls, it or they are removed from the court and considered dead and play continues.

Section 3 - Illegal Movement of an Opponent's Ball - If a player moves one or more of his/her opponent's balls, those balls will be awarded one point each and play continues. Only the team fouled against can be awarded points that frame.

Section 4 - Illegal Movement of the Pallino by a Player - If the pallino is moved by a player:

  a) The team that is fouled will be awarded as many points as the number of live balls that they have already played and the frame will end or

  b) The team that was fouled may have the option of declining the penalty and completing the frame.

ARTICLE 3 - Accidental or Premature Movement of Balls or Pallino by Referee

Section 1 - Accidental Movement of a Ball or Pallino During Play - (when more balls are yet to be played) - If a referee, either in the course of measuring or otherwise moves the pallino or a ball "in contention," the frame is dead and started over at the same end.

Section 2 - Accidental or Premature Movement of a Ball or Pallino by a Referee After All Balls Are Played - If the point or points were obvious to the referee, they will be awarded. All uncertain points will not be awarded.

ARTICLE 4 - Interference with a Ball in Motion

Section 1 - By One's Own Team - If a player interferes with his/her team's ball in motion, that team automatically forfeits the ball and play continues. If balls in play are disrupted as a result, it will be considered an illegal movement of the ball. The rules for illegal movement will apply.

Section 2 - By Opponent's Team - If a player interferes with an opponent's ball in motion, the team that is fouled has the option of:

  a) playing the ball over

  b) declaring the frame dead

  c) declining the penalty and accepting the position of the ball and continuing to play

Section 3 - With No Disruption of Position - If a spectator, animal or object such as a stick or stone interferes with a ball in motion and it does not touch another ball already in play, it must be played over by the same player.

Section 4 - With Disruption of Position - If a spectator, animal or object such as a stick or stone interferes with a ball in motion and that ball touches another ball already in play, the frame is dead.

Section 5 - Other Disruption of Play - Any action which interferes with the position of the ball(s) in play - renders the frame dead. Such action may be the result of, for example: a dead ball, foreign objects, spectators, or animals entering the court and changing the position of the ball(s) in play.

ARTICLE 5 - Wrong Color Delivery

Section 1 - Replaceable - If a player delivers a wrong color ball, the ball may not be stopped by another player or the referee. The ball must be allowed to come to rest and be replaced with the proper ball by the referee.

Section 2 - Not Replaceable - If a player delivers a wrong color ball that cannot be replaced without disturbing another ball already in play, the points of the play will be recorded at that time, with the wrong color ball counting for the team which rolled it, and play will continue.

Section 3 - Unidentifiable - If a player delivers a wrong color ball which cannot be identified by the referee as a result of hitting or scattering of balls, the frame will be considered dead and no points awarded.

ARTICLE 6 - Wrong Rotation of Play

Section 1 - Initial Roll - If a team wrongly delivers the pallino and its first ball, the referee will return both pallino and the ball and begin the frame over again.

Section 2 - If a player rolls out of turn, the opposing team may leave everything, including the thrown ball exactly as is, or may return any moved balls to their approximate previous positions and remove the thrown ball.

Section 3 - If an individual delivers more than his allotted number of balls, the opposing team may accept the result of the illegal roll, or remove the illegal ball and return any scattered balls to their original positions.

RULE 7: OTHER CIRCUMSTANCES

ARTICLE 1 - Broken Ball

Section 1 - During Play - If during the course of play of a frame, a ball or pallino breaks, the frame will be considered dead. Replacement of the ball or pallino will be the responsibility of the Tournament Directors.

Section 2 - Ball Pickup - To avoid wrong ball delivery the court should be cleared of balls at the end of every frame. The balls should be given to the appropriate players and a quiet, visual inspection made by the referee before the next frame begins again. The balls should be held by the players until it is their turn to deliver them.

RULE 8: THE OFFICIAL

ARTICLE 1 - Responsibilities

The Referee Shall:

Section 1 - Inspect the court before each game to insure proper grooming and safety.

Section 2 - Check the scoreboard and scorecard for accuracy.

Section 3 - Inspect the scorecard for team lineup before the game begins.

Section 4 - Call all fouls and determine all penalties according to the rules.

Section 5 - Dress in appropriate attire. The official should wear a yellow vest and cap when officiating a game.

ARTICLE 2 - Objections

Section 1 - Objections to Officials - Each team has the right to object to a designated official for any reason prior to the start of a game. This objection shall be considered and decided upon by the Tournament Directors.

ARTICLE 3 - Substitution of Officials

Section 1 - During a Game - Substitutions of officials may occur during a game only with the permission of the Tournament Directors and both coaches.

Section 2 - Additional officials may be assigned to any games during the course of play, provided permission is granted by the Tournament Directors.

Chapter 9

International Play

Bocce is becoming increasingly more visible as a competitive, international sport. Enthusiasts were disappointed when the host city, Barcelona, selected jai-alai over bocce as a demonstration sport for the 1992 Summer Olympics. Bocce again flirted with Olympic exhibition sport status in Atlanta in 1996. Many anticipate that it will finally reach that level in Sydney, Australia in the year 2000. The International Olympic Committee (I.O.C.) has officially recognized the sport, and this is a major step toward becoming an Olympic medal sport.

There are two sets of rules approved for true international play (not including Special Olympics rules discussed below). In Punto, Raffa, Volo Rules, the three different shots are legal if executed according to the regulations, but in Volo Rules only the volo and punto shots are allowed. The first thing international tournament competitors want to know is whether the event is governed by Raffa (meaning punto, raffa, volo) or Volo Rules (volo and punto shots only, and usually played with metal balls). The international court is a large one, 27.5 x 4 meters (approximately 90.2 x 13.1 feet) for Volo play. For Punto, Raffa, Volo competition, the court may be 24 to 26.5 meters long and 3.8 to 4.5 meters wide (approximately 78.7 to 86.9 feet long and 12.5 to 14.8 feet wide).

International rules are more complicated than open rules, but experienced players maintain that the regulations are not intimidating once you get acclimated to the style of play. The international game is for purists. They want to remove the element of luck from bocce. For example, you try to knock your opponents' point away with a volo attempt, and your shot is off target, hitting your own ball instead. This results, by chance, in your team winning the point. Purists reason, why should you gain an advantage after making a poor shot? By international rules, if your ball didn't land within a specified distance of its target, it may be removed from play, and all balls disrupted by the volo attempt returned to their original positions. Like in the rules for other major sports, there is a rule of advantage option. Simply stated, if your opponent makes an illegal play that benefits your team, you have the option of accepting the result of the play.

In international games, referees mark the positions of live balls and, not unlike billiards, players call their shots. The balls' positions are marked in case a player attempts a knockaway shot and misses, displacing other balls in the process. Those balls may be returned to their original positions, which were previously marked on the court surface. Referees use a specialized measuring device to mark the positions of balls and to trace arcs on the court surface. These arcs serve as boundaries for legal landing points for volo shots. As you might guess, these games take a lot longer than those played with Open Rules. International volo competitions sometimes set a time limit for each contest, which may last from two to three hours. Critics of international style play claim that it is too complicated and makes the game too long and dull. The American people will prefer a quick and simple game, they maintain. And if a pro bocce tour ever comes to fruition, television coverage will demand a fast-paced, action-packed game. Purists counter that, when bocce enters the Olympic arena, international rules will prevail. Americans should learn the game on the large court and with the rules that will allow them to pursue the dream of one day representing the United States in international competition. To this end, Donna Allen of the USBF, strongly recommends that any schools constructing courts should build them to international specifications. "Build a backyard court to whatever dimensions fit your on your property and make you happy," she advises. "But build international-sized courts in the schools, and give our young people the opportunity to represent their country."

Restrictions in Punto, Raffa, Volo & Volo Play

If, when rolling for point in Punto, Raffa, Volo competition, your ball hits another ball and that ball travels more than 70 cm (about 28 inches) from its original location, the roll is not valid. For Volo play this distance is 1 meter (about 39 inches). The referee will apply what is called the rule of advantage. Your opponent gets the option of a) directing the referee to put all the displaced balls back in their original positions, and remove from play the ball that you rolled, or b) leaving everything in place including the ball that you just rolled (the displacement of balls caused by your roll may represent an advantage for your opponent, so in a sense, he can decline the penalty). In Volo play the ball you rolled would be removed from play even in option b.

When attempting a raffa, you must declare the target (any ball, including your own or the pallino). Your shot must hit the declared target or any other ball (including pallino) within 13 cm (about 5 inches) of that target. Again, a shot that does not meet the requirements of a valid raffa results in invoking the rule of advantage.

For a proper volo shot in Punto, Raffa, Volo regulations, you must inform the referee of your intent, including which ball is your target. You must wait for the official to trace a 40 cm arc (about 16 inches) in front of the target. To be valid, the volo attempt must strike any ball (including the pallino) within 13 cm of the declared target, and it must first strike the ground within 40 cm of the struck ball. A volo that lands on the line delimiting the traced arc is invalid. The arc traced in Volo Regulations is 50 cm and the restrictions are the same as for Punto, Raffa, Volo play except you cannot call your own ball. Also, unless you designate the pallino as the target, a displaced pallino is always returned to its previous position whether or not the volo shot was valid. No matter how the balls are scattered by the called shot, we can tell by the arcs if the ball fulfills the necessary requirements. The referee can check the mark left by the ball when it struck ground. If the ball struck a ball on the fly, the referee can check the marked position of the ball that was struck.

The Shoot-Out & Rapid Fire Shoot-out

Some international competitions feature shoot-outs not unlike the NBA three-point shoot-out. Officials place balls in different positions and at different distances from the shooter. The balls are side by side, one in front of another, even behind the pallino. Points are awarded for successful hits based on the degree of difficulty for the particular shot. For this Precision Shooting, players generally shoot twice at each target, proceeding in a predetermined sequence, and keep a cumulative score. There are even rapid-fire shoot-outs where players run from one end of the court to the other attempting to score as many hits as possible within a five-minute time limit.

This bocce facility in Campione, Switzerland, has seating for 2000 people. (Photo courtesy of the United States Bocce Federation)

A Summary of the Punto, Raffa, Volo Regulations of the Confederation Boccistica Internationale

(This unofficial summary of the C.B.I. regulations was prepared by the United States Bocce Federation. It is intended only to be an abbreviated guide to the most frequently used rules. Any questions must be resolved by using the complete text of the official C.B.I. regulations.)

I. The Court (See court diagram)

A line = backwall.

B line = where you roll bocce or shoot raffa.

C line = where you shoot volo. Also a raffa shot (from B line) must first hit ground after C line. Further, a player rolling a bocce cannot pass the C line unless he is out of balls.

D line = pallino must be tossed beyond (and before B line). Also, player who has shot raffa or volo cannot pass D line.

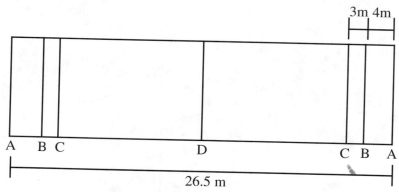

II. The Match

Each match consists of three games. First you play three against three with each player having two balls. Next you play a singles game with each player having four balls. Finally, you play a doubles and again each player has two balls. A substitution can be made at any time after a ball has been played. However, there are no substitutions in the singles game and no player can participate in more that two of the three games in the match. Normally games go to 15 points.

III. Starting the Match

A. The Beginning

1. Each game of a match begins with the referee placing the pallino in the center of the court between the B & D lines. The winners of the coin toss may play the first bocce or choose the end from which to begin. If the first bocce played is invalid, the same team must play again until they have played a valid ball.

B. The Pallino

1. During the game the jack is tossed by the winner of the previous round. If the toss is invalid the opponent tosses the pallino. If that is also invalid, the pallino is placed in the center of the court between the B & D lines. In any event, the first bocce is played by the team that first tossed the pallino. You should always wait for the assent of the referee before tossing the pallino. The pallino toss is valid if it passes (not touches) the D line, stops below (not on or after) the B line and does not touch or stop within 13 cm of the sideboard. If after a valid play, the pallino moves in front of or on the D line, or the pallino leaves the court, the play stops and is resumed from the opposite end.

IV. Punto, Raffa, Volo

A. Punto

1. When pointing, a player's foot may be on but not over the B line.

2. A ball that hits the side wall without first hitting another object is invalid. After stopping, the Rule of Advantage is determined by the opposing team.

3. If there is a tie for point, the team last playing plays again until the tie is broken.

4. If the rolled ball hits another ball which travels more than 70 cm, everything returns to its original position and the rolled ball is thrown out or everything including the rolled ball remains in place. It makes no difference how far the rolled ball travels. If several balls are moved and no single object travels more than 70 cm, everything is valid. If the rolled ball hits an object causing the object to hit the side or back wall, everything is valid unless the object hit traveled more than 70 cm (measured from original mark to position when stopped).

B. Raffa

1. The raffa shot must be made from the B line and the ball must first touch the ground after the C line.

2. Before taking a raffa shot you must inform the referee that you intend to raffa and which object is your target.

3. If the raffa is invalid, the opposing team may leave everything including the thrown ball as is or replace everything and remove the thrown ball.

4. The raffa shot must be released before the player's foot goes over the B line (on the line is valid).

5. To be valid the raffa shot must first hit the declared target or any object within 13 cm of the target.

6. You may raffa any ball including your own or the pallino.

C. Volo

1. Before taking a volo shot you must inform the referee that you intend to volo, which is your target and wait for the referee to mark a 40 cm arch in front of the target.

2. The volo shot is valid if it strikes any object within 13 cm of the declared target and the shot hits the ground within 40 cm of the struck ball.

3. If the volo shot is invalid, the opposing team may leave everything including the thrown ball as is or replace everything and remove the thrown ball.

4. The volo shot must be released before the player's foot goes over the C line (on the line is valid).

5. You may volo any ball including your own or the pallino.

● **ROLLED OR THROWN BALL**   – – – – – – **PATH OF ROLLED OR THROWN BALL**

○ **HIT BALL**   — — — **PATH OF 1st HIT BALL**

—————— **PATH OF 2nd HIT BALL**

Punto Shot

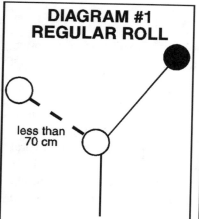

DIAGRAM #1
REGULAR ROLL

less than 70 cm

When the rolled ball moves an object less than 70 cm everything is valid, no matter how far the rolled ball travels and even if it hits the sidewall.

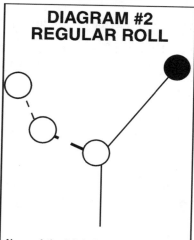

DIAGRAM #2
REGULAR ROLL

None of the hit balls traveled over 70 cm so everything is valid.

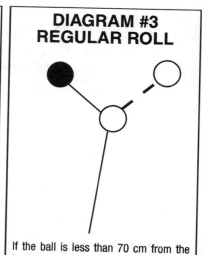

DIAGRAM #3
REGULAR ROLL

If the ball is less than 70 cm from the back board, the play is always regular.

Raffa Shot

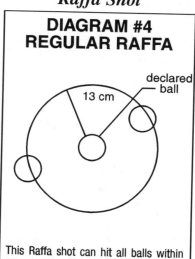

DIAGRAM #4
REGULAR RAFFA

declared ball

13 cm

This Raffa shot can hit all balls within 13 cm of the declared ball.

Volo Shot

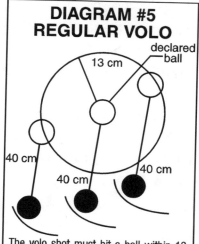

DIAGRAM #5
REGULAR VOLO

declared ball

13 cm

40 cm

40 cm

40 cm

The volo shot must hit a ball within 13 cm of the declared target and the ground inside a 40 cm arc of the hit ball.

A Summary of the Volo Regulations of the Fédération International de Boules

(This unofficial summary of the F.I.B. regulations was prepared by the United States Bocce Federation. It is intended only to be an abbreviated guide to the most frequently used rules. Any questions must be resolved by using the complete text of the official F.I.B. regulations.)

I. Starting the Game

The right to the first toss of the jack is chosen by coin flip. The toss of the jack is valid if it comes to rest in the designated square at the opposite end of the court (i.e., between the A & B lines).

If a team fails to validly toss the jack after two attempts, the opposing team places the jack where it wishes within the square as long as it is at least 50 cm from all boundary lines of the square.

In any event, the first bocce is rolled by the team that first tossed the jack. The opposing team then plays until they take the point or play all their balls. If the first ball goes out of play, the opposing team rolls the next ball. If their ball also goes out of play the first team plays again and so on. If no balls are left on the court after a valid roll or throw, the opposing team must play.

II. Rolling the Bocce

If a rolled ball hits another ball or the jack causing that hit ball or jack to move more than one meter it is an irregular play. The opposing team may move all balls back to their original positions or they may leave everything in its new position. In either case, the ball rolled is thrown out (see diagram 1).

If a rolled ball hits another ball or the jack and the hit ball does not move more than one meter but the rolled ball does move more than one meter it is an irregular play. The opposing team may move all the balls back to their original positions or they may leave everything in its new position. In either case the rolled ball remains where it stopped (see diagram 2).

Any ball striking a side wall is thrown out unless it its the result of an irregular play (see diagrams 4, 5 & 6). A rolled ball that comes to rest on a sideline is valid only if at least 1/2 of the ball is still in the playing area (see diagram 10).

When each team has a ball equidistant from the jack, the team that rolled last plays again. If the tie is not broken, the other team plays and so forth until the tie is broken.

If you play someone else's ball by mistake, simply replace it with the correct ball.

III. Shooting the Bocce

When shooting volo, the ball must land within a 50 cm arc of the designated target or it is an irregular shot. If the thrown ball lands on the arc, it is irregular. The opposing team may then move all the bocce balls back to their original position or leave all the bocce balls in their new positions. The thrown ball is taken out (see diagrams 7, 8 & 9).

A team cannot designate one of its own balls.

IV. Shooting the Bocce

If a team chooses to shoot the jack, the jack must be declared and marked with a 50 cm. arch.

In the case of a valid or irregular shot with a non-declared jack, the jack, if moved, must always return to its original position.

In the case of an irregular shot with a declared jack the opposing team may move everything back to its original position or accept everything that resulted from the irregular shot.

If a declared jack is shot out of play after a valid shot with both teams still having balls to play, the round is over and it is repeated from the same end. The team that last tossed the jack does so again.

If a declared jack is shot out of play after a valid shot and only one team has balls remaining, that team receives one point for each ball that has not yet been played.

V. Position of Players

In all cases, when it is not their turn to play, the players must stand to the side of the square where the jack is positioned, one team on each side of the court. When an opposing player is shooting, other players must remain still and do nothing to distract the shooting player.

VI. Referee

The decision of the referee is final.

● **ROLLED OR THROWN BALL**
○ **HIT BALL**

– – – – – . **PATH OF ROLLED OR THROWN BALL**
– – – **PATH OF 1st HIT BALL**
————— **PATH OF 2nd HIT BALL**

Rolling the Bocce

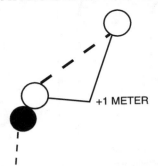

DIAGRAM #1
IRREGULAR ROLL

+1 METER

Rolled (black) ball hits other ball and moves it more than one meter. Rolled ball is thrown out and hit ball can be put back or left where it is.

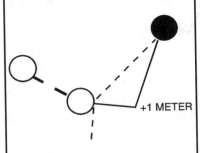

DIAGRAM #2
IRREGULAR ROLL

+1 METER

Rolled (black) ball hits other ball which moves less than one meter but rolled ball moves more than one meter. Rolled ball stays and hit ball can be put back or left where it is.

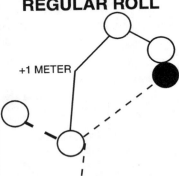

DIAGRAM #3
REGULAR ROLL

+1 METER

Rolled (black) ball hits 1st ball less than 1 meter, then hits 2nd ball less than 1 meter. Everything is valid because no single object traveled more than 1 meter.

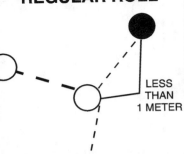

DIAGRAM #4
REGULAR ROLL

LESS THAN 1 METER

Rolled (black) ball hits other ball into wall (or over sideline) and then moves less than one meter. Rolled ball is valid. Ball hitting wall is out. You don't measure ball that hits wall or crosses sideline.

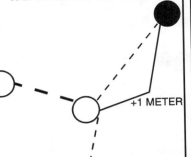

DIAGRAM #5
IRREGULAR ROLL

+1 METER

Rolled (black) ball hits other ball into wall (or over sideline) and then moves more than one meter. Rolled ball stays and hit ball can be put back or thrown out.

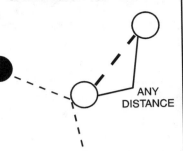

DIAGRAM #6
IRREGULAR ROLL

ANY DISTANCE

Rolled (black) ball hits other ball and then hits wall (or over sideline). Hit ball moves any distance. Hit ball can be put back or left where it is. Rolled ball is thrown out.

Shooting the Bocce

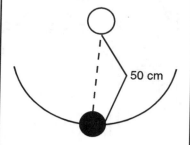

DIAGRAM #7 IRREGULAR ROLL

50 cm

Thrown (black) ball is irregular because it broke the 50 cm arc. Thrown ball goes out. All hit balls can be put back or left where they are.

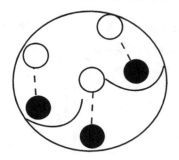

DIAGRAM #8 ALL VALID SHOTS

All balls within 50 cm of designated target can be marked with an arc. To be valid, thrown ball must hit within 50 cm of designated target and within 50 cm of ball actually hit.

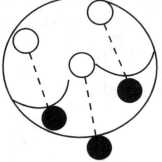

DIAGRAM #9 ALL IRREGULAR SHOTS

All balls within 50 cm of designated target can be marked with an arc. To be valid, thrown ball must hit within 50 cm of designated target and within 50 cm of ball actually hit.

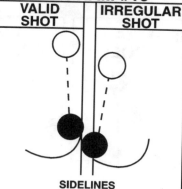

DIAGRAM #10

VALID SHOT	IRREGULAR SHOT

SIDELINES

If thrown ball (black) lands on the sideline at least 1/2 of it must have been in the playing area.

Special Olympics World Games

In 1995, New Haven, Connecticut played host to 500,000 people for the Special Olympics World Summer Games. More than 7000 athletes, and teams from 140 countries gathered there with 30 countries competing in bocce. Bocce Commissioner Marie Bedard, along with tireless assistants Jack Hogan and Roger Lord, did yeoman work assembling a bocce committee and putting together a first-class competition. Since rules standardization was not yet a reality, the committee had to select a set of rules to govern play, create a certification process for bocce officials, and then recruit volunteers for training and certification. The committee selected the IBA (International Bocce Association, address listed on Chapter 5) rules as the official regulations governing play. These are closer to Open Rules than they are to true international rules. A few friends of mine and I jumped at the opportunity to become part of the Special Olympics World Games. We made regular trips to Waterbury, Connecticut where we learned the IBA rules and officiating mechanics, and worked with Special Olympians. We not only became bocce officials in good standing, but we shared a very special experience with truly special athletes. Seven thousand adult and child athletes with mental retardation represented the 140 countries. There were gala opening and closing ceremonies at the Yale Bowl, a parade of tall ships, and numerous festivals and cultural activities. President and Mrs. Clinton opened the games, and celebrities from Arnold Schwarzenegger to super-model Kathy Ireland made appearances.

The Special Olympics movement continues to change the way society views people with mental and physical disabilities. There are no head starts, no "do-overs," no special time-outs. These athletes have the same opportunities and hardships as any other people participating in high-level competitions.

The Special Olympics Summer Games represented the largest sporting event on the planet in 1995. This is particularly impressive when you ponder the program's modest beginnings. Started in 1963 by Eunice Kennedy Shriver, it was a summer day camp for people with mental retardation. She hosted the first event in her backyard in Rockville, Maryland, and the competitors ranged from age 8 to 80. Just five years later, the first World Games were held at Soldier Field in Chicago with 1000 athletes from 26 states and Canada competing. Today, Special Olympics chapters are operating in all 50 states and 145 countries.

Besides bocce, this most recent World Games competition included aquatics, athletics (track & field), badminton, basketball, bowling, cycling, equestrian events, football (soccer), golf, gymnastics, power weightlifting, rollerskating, sailing, softball, table tennis, team handball, tennis, and volleyball. Many of the events included unified teams — events that pair Special Olympians with athletes without mental retardation.

Bocce first became a World Games event in 1991 with 41 athletes competing. The summer of 1995 saw 151 athletes take part in singles, doubles, unified and other bocce events. There were teams from all over the world including South Africa, New Zealand, Bahamas, Bermuda, Jamaica, France, Iceland, Spain, Switzerland, Lebanon, and the United States. It is obvious that the number of bocce participants will continue to mushroom in the future. The sport is as well suited for the Special Olympics as it is for backyard lawn games and advanced tournament play. If you can roll a ball, you can play. We witnessed athletes with various degrees of physical and mental handicaps who competed extremely well. One bocce player was legally blind. Sporting a pair of binoculars strapped around his neck, he first lined up the shot peering through the binoculars. Then he let them hang from his neck as he tossed the ball. Releasing the shot, he again reached for the binoculars to track the ball to its target.

For the first time, people with mental retardation served among the more than 50 officials for the bocce competition. More than 600 dedicated volunteers ran the event, coordinating game times, officials, bus schedules, meals and everything else involved in an event of such magnitude. It was an uplifting experience seeing so many selfless people in one place, generously giving of themselves. According to what we heard from other officials and spectators, the same was true at the other sports venues (approximately 45,000 volunteers in all). The positive atmosphere and harmony that pervaded the events proved that these special athletes not only bring out their best talent for world class competition...they bring out the best in all those around them.

Special Olympics Oath

Let me win.

But if I cannot win

Let me be brave in the attempt.

Chapter 10
A Brief History Lesson ▬▬▬▬▬▬▬▬▬

(Relax — there won't be a test)

Bocce is an ancient game, its origin and evolution obscured by the mists of antiquity. The waters are further muddied by the fact that its development is intertwined with that of other bowling games. It is often unclear whether a historical reference refers to lawn bowls, bocce, or bowling. The more I attempted to research the history of bocce, the more I realized that there is no definitive history of the sport. What follows is less a history than a mixture of fact, conjecture, lore, and outright guess (don't look for footnotes and references). The lack of detailed documentation, however, makes the tale no less fascinating or intriguing.

Sir Flinders Petrie, emeritus professor of Egyptology at the University of London, unearthed an Egyptian tomb from 5200 BC bearing evidence of a bowling game played by young boys tossing balls or polished stones. Other Egyptian wall paintings and vases also appear to depict bocce-like games in progress. Some historians have gone as far as to call bocce the ancestor of all ball games.

It is believed that thousands of years ago inhabitants of Pharaoh's Egypt became the first bocce players (it must have been a welcome diversion from stacking pyramid stones). Later, Roman legionnaires played with naturally rounded rocks or perhaps coconuts brought back from African campaigns (it must have been a welcome diversion from stacking corpses of the conquered). Bocce may have derived from an ancient Greek exercise of throwing balls of varying size for distance. This sound mind, sound body ideal of the Greeks was right up the alley of the Romans, who modified the activity, tossing and rolling the balls along the ground toward a stationary target.

Bocce spread throughout the Middle East and Asia. Historians believe that the Greeks latched onto the game at around 600 BC (as evidenced in the painting and sculpture of the period) and introduced it to the Romans. The Romans probably took it on the road via their world conquest and spread the game Johnny Appleseed style. During breaks in the Punic Wars, soldiers selected a small stone "leader" and threw it first. Then they rolled, tossed, or heaved larger stones, with those coming closest to the leader scoring points. All of this appears to have been easy exercise and a pleasant change of pace from the stress of battle.

The Egyptian game became bocce in Italy, and was altered slightly to become boules in France and lawn bowls in England. It is easy to imagine the early games being played with spherical rocks or even coconuts (later, artisans would use hard olive wood to carve out balls). The name bocce is derived from the Italian bacio meaning kiss. The idea is to kiss, snuggle, or otherwise get close to the object of your affection — the pallino.

Eventually, people from all walks of life played bocce and bowls. The young, the old, men, women, scientists, artists, royalty — people of all stations enjoyed the sport. It is said that Caesar Augustus was partial to the game. Some medical experts even suggested that playing the game prevented rheumatism. In 1319 AD, King Charles IV of France banned bowl games for all but the nobility, because it supposedly diverted attention from more important tasks such as preparing for war and practicing archery. Edward III of England followed suit in 1361. In 1511 King Henry VIII imposed a similar ban on his subjects' (commoners and soldiers) lawn bowls. He reasoned that the activity might divert attention from archery (necessary for national defense) and lead to gambling and moray decay. A further act of 1541, not repealed until 1845, forbade commoners to play except on Christmas (and then only in their masters' houses and in their presence).

By 1519 bowling games became public diversions played in Flanders, Holland, and Belgium. As we have seen, the games were banned at various times in Italy, France, and England and were once even condemned by the Catholic Church citing a "pernicious gambling influence." Clearly, legislation failed to kill or seriously subdue interest in the sports. They flourished into Elizabeth's reign where bowls assumed prominent social status. Over time however, bowl games became increasingly associated with taverns, drinking, and gambling and became unfashionable.

In 1658 one Puritan offered the following confession after succumbing to the temptation of forbidden bowling:

"To those concerned, I hereby say, I should not make confessions which are likely to be read from this page at some future time by public eyes but my conscience is troubling me, so I seek this way to ease it. The weather is tantalizing warm, but I was tempted to do what I have refrained from doing before. This game of bowls has bewitched me, I fear. For I played it today and for funds. Yet, I was fortunate, for the bet was 10. Woe unto me! My fellow Puritans will be shocked if they hear of this, but the more reason for my confession. I like the game, my own ability to win, and the fine folks I met on the greens. May this confession do my soul good."

Excerpted from The Complete Handbook of Bowling *by Oscar Fraley. Prentice-Hall, Inc., 1959.*

The ball games' lore suggests that Sir Francis Drake, when told of the rapidly advancing Spanish Armada, insisted on finishing his game before setting out to resist the enemy. And Italian lore has it that playing bocce in the streets resulted in bruises to the legs of passing noblemen. This served to bring much attention to the sport among Italian nobility, and led to it becoming a favorite pastime of the aristocracy. Giusseppe Garibaldi, who is more widely known for unifying and nationalizing Italy, is also credited with popularizing the sport as it is known today. Bocce had its ups and downs historically — periodically gaining and losing popularity. In 1896, the first Olympiad was held in Athens, Greece. Bocce hit the international scene then and is holding on tenaciously today.

When Italian immigrants brought their game to America in the late 19th and early 20th centuries, it was a regionalized version of the activity. Just as there are similar yet somewhat different dialects throughout any country, there were similar yet varying ways of playing bocce. Each court constructed in the United States met the specifications of those used in the immigrants' area of the "old country." Similarly, each area used the regionalized rules from their part of Italy. Bocce is and has remained a remarkably resilient game, surviving and growing despite these problems.

Spectators have always taken to the sport, with kibitzers seemingly a necessary element of bocce. Everybody seems to have an idea of how the next shot should proceed, and few are reluctant to share their counsel. It is reminiscent of the classic *Mad Magazine* spoof on Little League baseball. As a youngster is sprinting toward third base, the parents and coaches are wildly calling out instructions. "Score, Score, Score!" says one adult. "No — Stop, Stop, Stop at third!" calls out another. "Go Back to second!" orders yet another. "Tag up! Tag up! Tag up!" and "Slide! Slide! Slide!" are still other commands from the stands. Like Little League parents, bocce's armchair generals are evidence of the game's abiding appeal.

In Italy and in the early days of bocce in the United States, women and children were discouraged from playing. This game was the domain of men. It may have begun to die out because men did not share it with women and the younger generation. Its resurgence today is due to the fact that play is no longer confined to Italian adult males. It has moved beyond its ethnic roots and has become a game for all people of all ages. A movement is on today to construct courts in public parks. This is a major step toward spreading the game to more and more Americans. Extending the game from the private sector (social clubs that require membership fees) to the public sector also provides the opportunity to get outdoors and play in the fresh air with family and friends. In Martinez, California, home of the United States Bocce Federation, outdoor courts are well established. You can even get pizza delivered to your court by telephoning and specifying your court number.

Played in Italy since before the Caesars, bocce has survived the Fall of the Roman Empire and the threat of fascism. It has evolved to a tournament sport carrying ever-increasing cash prizes and luring corporate sponsors. Undoubtedly it will thrive and continue to flourish. This is testimony to the enduring appeal of an activity that evolved in different parts of the world, is played somewhat differently from country to country, yet whose basic idea is the same. Let's see who can roll, toss, or otherwise deliver their bocce balls closest to the object ball. Bocce, played widely today in Italy, Australia, South America, and other countries, is about to explode in the United States.

A Word on Bowls — also called Lawn Bowling

"What sport shall we devise here in this garden, to drive away the heavy thought of care?" Queen Isabella queries in Shakespeare's Richard II. "Madam, we'll play at bowls," responds her handmaid. Lawn bowls is a ball-and-target game similar to bocce, in that players roll balls toward a stationary object, but is played on a closely cropped grass lawn without side and end boards. The eight- to ten-ounce jack is rolled down the course and competitors use three-pound bowls made of wood, rubber, or composition material to try to score points. These bowls are not round but biased; they are elliptical and weighted on one side. The weighting was originally accomplished by loading the ball with lead, but now is done by making one side more convex than the other. When rolled, this bias causes the ball to curve like a tenpin bowling ball (perhaps lawn bowls is the precursor of that game). An interesting wrinkle to this game is that as each ball is delivered, the player's rear foot must be on or above a small, strategically placed mat.

New York's Bowling Green is a reminder that bowls was an important recreation for early settlers. George Washington's dad built a bowling green at Mt. Vernon in 1732, and the game enjoyed great popularity until the Revolutionary War, after which it became dormant for the next 100 years or so. George Vanderbilt and John D. Rockefeller had private bowling greens on their estates, and Walt Disney hosted bowling friends at his Palm Springs home.

Lawn Bowls

A Word on Boules (also called Pétanque)

Boules, jeu de boules, or pétanque are names for the French version of bowls or bocce. Although the game is played in many countries, boules is as closely associated with France as bullfighting is with Spain. It is usually played on sand or gravel with metal balls that are smaller than bocce or lawn bowls. Like bowls, the game is played without side or end boards on an area called a pitch. The object ball (beut or cochonnet) is so small (on the order of a table tennis ball) that the game is difficult to play on grass. Even closely cropped lawns tend to obliterate it from view. As in lawn bowls, the rules require players to take their shots from a designated area (often both feet within a circle drawn or painted on the ground).

A Classic Case of One-Ups-Manship

The three ball-and-target games of bocce, boules, and bowls are classic contests of one-ups-manship. If you can roll the ball six inches away from the target, I can draw to within five. Such activities have had enormous appeal, especially with the element of strategy and team competition added to the mix. And 7000 years of staying power is a pretty good endorsement. If we consider bocce, boules, and bowls variations of the same game, that game must be classified as one of the largest participatory sports in the world today.

These photos show the size of the metal ball used in boules and the technique of tossing volo-style into the air.

Get in Shape with Masters Press!

SportsLog Series

A collection of logs designed to help athletes keep better track of their workouts. Each log includes 56 undated weeks of calendar pages (two full pages per week); a 25-page training and nutritional guide, and color photos with inspirational quotes. There are logs for walking, running, cycling, weightlifting, triathlon training, each priced at $9.95.

ISBN NUMBERS
WalkLog   1-57028-053-3
RunLog   1-57028-055-X
CycleLog 1-57028-057-6
TriLog   1-57028-054-1
LiftLog   1-57028-056-8

Kinesiology of Exercise
Michael Yessis, Ph.D.
The most authoritative book available on how body building/weight training exercises can be performed for maximum effectiveness and safety. $17.95, ISBN 0-940279-36-3

Fitness Walking
Scott Roberts, Ph.D.
Join America's latest fitness craze by learning how to build endurance, lose weight, increase energy and feel better about yourself through walking.
$14.95, ISBN 1-57028-034-7

Your Injury:
A Common Sense Guide to Sports Injuries
Merrill A. Ritter, M.D. & Marjorie J. Albohm, A.T., C.
An essential reference for amateur athletes who want to prevent, treat or recover from sports injuries.
$14.95, ISBN 1-57028-011-8

WALKLOG
Diary & Guide for the Exercise Walker
1st Edition
Don & Debbi Lawrence

LIFTLOG
Diary & Guide for Strength Training
1st Edition
Nate Foster/Tim Houts

TRILOG
Diary & Guide for the Triathlete & Duathlete
4th Edition
Tim Houts/Jan Bass

RUNLOG
Diary & Guide for the Runner
3rd Edition
Tim Houts-John Cronin

CYCLELOG
Diary & Guide for the Cyclist
2nd Edition
Tim Houts/Jan Bass

Call Toll Free 1-800-9-SPORTS To Order

Hit a Home Run with Masters Press!

Masters Press has a complete line of books on baseball and soft-ball, and other sports to help coaches and participants alike "master their game."

All of our books are available at better bookstores or by calling Masters Press at 1-800-9-SPORTS. Catalogs available by request.

Defensive Baseball
Rod Delmonico

Position-by-position as well as overall team strategies are presented in a concise, easy to understand format. Its photos and illustrations make this one of the best visual-aid instructional baseball books available.
$14.95, ISBN 1-57028-029-0

Heads-Up Baseball: Playing the Game One Pitch at a Time
Tom Hanson & Ken Ravizza

"This book provides practical strategies for developing the mental skills which will help speed you to your full potential."

— *Dave Winfield*
(Introduction by Jim Abbott and foreword by Hank Aaron)
$14.95, ISBN 1-57028-021-5

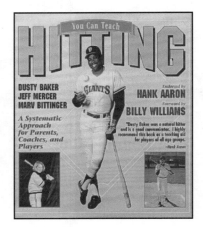

You Can Teach Hitting
Dusty Baker with Jeff Mercer & Marv Bittinger

Written by the acclaimed manager of the San Francisco Giants, this book is lavishly illustrated with four-color photographs and computer enhanced graphics throughout, and takes you from selecting your bat to selecting your pitch.
$24.95, ISBN 0-940279-73-8

Youth League Baseball
Skip Bertman

Skip Bertman, coach of the 1994 NCAA Champion LSU Tigers, devotes each chapter to a specific phase of the game. Includes information on basic skills such as hitting and catching, as well as on more complex matters such as position-specific abilities. Part of the Spalding Youth League Series.
$12.95, ISBN 0-940279-68-1

Softball: Fast and Slow Pitch
Mario Pagnoni & Gerald Robinson

Designed to help improve individual and team performance, this book includes information on team warm-ups, position-specific drills and equipment selection.
$12.95, ISBN 1-57028-025-8

Call Toll Free 1-800-9-SPORTS To Order